I0111429

THE VISITOR

A Play in Two Acts

By

Thomas Alexander

The Visitor by Thomas Alexander

Direct Light Publishing
45 Dudley Court, Endell Street, London, WC2H 9RF

Copyright © 2014 Thomas Alexander. All rights reserved.

No part of this publication may be reproduced or transmitted in any form or by any means, electronic or mechanical, including photocopy, recording, performance, any information storage and retrieval system, without permission in writing from the publisher.

For Worldwide Performance Rights please contact Thomas Alexander at Direct Light Productions
thomasalexander@directlight-publications.com

Permissions may be sought directly from:
Publishing Rights Department, 45 Dudley Court, Endell Street, London, WC2H 9RF
Email:
Library of Congress Cataloguing in Publication Data
Application submitted.
British Library Cataloguing in Publication Data
Application submitted.
03 04 05 06 07 08 09 8 7 6 5 4 3 2 1 0
uuid:6452fce2-cd8b-440b-8205-8a7a1a32ea04
ISBN: 978-1-941979-04-4

–

The characters and events in this book are fictitious. Any similarity to real persons, living or dead, is coincidental and unintended by the author.

Copyright © 2012 Thomas Alexander

All rights reserved.

Edited by Shirin Laghai for Direct Light Publishing

Available in Ebook and Soft Cover from Direct Light

Cover design by SimplyA
© Direct Light Publications 2014

For Farzad
Who opened his oubliette

ABOUT THE AUTHOR

Thomas Alexander has worked in almost all forms of theatre, from opera to children's performances, working as everything from stage hand to costume designer, and has seen his work translated into four different languages and performed as far afield as America and Afghanistan.

His plays; *Writing William, Begat, Great, The Visitor* & *Murder Me Gently* along with his novel; *A Scattering Of Orphans* have been published by DIRECT LIGHT.

Also by the Author

PLAYS

Happiness
Murder Me Gently
The Family
Begat
The Crossroads Country
Great
The Visitor
When Dusk Brings Glory
The Recruitment Officer
Writer's Block
The Last Christmas
Writing William
The Big Match

NOVELS

A Scattering Of Orphans

ONE ACT PLAYS

Four Widows and A Funeral
For Arts Sake
The TV
Life TM
The Dance

ADAPTATIONS

William Shakespeare's' R3
Othello

THE VISITOR

Acknowledgements

Numerous people have been involved in drafts of the play presented here, some of whose names have been lost to the annuls of history.

Nevertheless, in Chronological order, I would like to thank Fiona Umetsu, Jane Batson, Gareth Williams, Hélène Salvini Fujita, Shirin Laghai, Adam Carpenter, Farzad Rafii

FOREWORD

By Thomas Alexander

The first shape The Visitor took was as a novel I started back in 1996. I had just moved to Tokyo, and I remember sitting and writing in a sunroom on the 8th floor of a building in the suburbs while a friend painted a mural on the wall behind me of… I forget what. I believe it had something to do with rainbows!

I have no idea why I gave up writing the novel. I'm sure that, as usual, life usurped art, and work overtook what was then just a hobby. I remember writing the scene, as described in the play, where the Poet sneaks over the border into the war-torn country in search of his lover and thinking that I liked it, but I'm not sure I got much further than that. I can't tell for sure because I had started writing the book on an old electronic word processor and, like most of my work pre-millennium, there was no way of getting it back once the machine went the way of the dodo, burning out in an electrical short while in Hong Kong a couple of years later.

Nevertheless, the story stayed with me. The debate between belief and aesthetics has been a long struggle for me, dating back to studying theology at university, and one I was eager to explore. Indeed, one of the earliest proofs of God I came up with during that time involved this dichotomy.

"Bees are attracted to flowers," the ill thought out proof began. "In fact, the entire design of a flower – the purpose of it – is to attract bees and other insects to aid in pollination. Humans, too, find flowers aesthetically pleasing, though not for the same reasons. Indeed, the aesthetic property of a flower could be seen as a design flaw when it comes to how humans use them, but nevertheless there it was, proving that aesthetics were the same across species and pointing to a design, rather than an accident of selection."

Even ignoring the possibility that the 'prime mover' in this case supports evolution as much as theism, the argument is flawed. One can ask about things that aren't attractive across multiple species, but nevertheless the position of love central to modern Christianity is still incongruous with the notion of fidelity. Or, to put it another way, how can so many flowers be so attractive! And I still felt that there was a lot of scope to the idea of putting faith in love as the bedrock of all human endeavours, as opposed to faith in the divine.

The plot, of course, took its own direction with that.

I'm not sure of the exact date when I first decided to turn The Visitor into a play. By that point I was solidly working and writing for theatre, and had no interest in spending a year on this question in the shape of a novel. I have no idea how long it took me to write the first draft of it as a play, but it was certainly no more than a week. All I remember is that I hated it! It was too purple. Too profound. Too self-righteous. And I didn't like any of the characters at all, which is always a bad sign for any writer. It went straight back into the drawer, which in my case was a hard-drive, filed along with the dozens of half-started half-finished and simply unloved manuscripts that cluttered up my documents folder.

In the summer of 2010, however, I was forced to revisit it.

I had a show on in London which we were thinking of moving to Paris, and the actor central to the production liked the idea of translating a small four-hander into French. She asked me if I had anything which fit the bill, and thinking that The Visitor would work well as a bilingual production I dug it up with the intention of giving it a new gloss of paint before sending it off.

The strange thing was that this time I liked it. And I liked the characters as well, especially The Jailor, who always seemed to me to be the only one with a moral compass, albeit a skewed one. And while the Paris translation never transpired, I spent a lot of time reworking it and fixing the more extravagant passages of dialogue.

To my mind the central premise of the play has always been has always been this:

What if David Hare was trapped in a room with Billy Graham, and they were both in love with the same woman?

Could the humanist allow the suffering of another without thwarting his own desires? Could a religious man cling to his martyrdom in the face of another man claiming the one he loved?

There are a number of romantics in the play, and I don't think that's such a bad thing. The character of The Missionary is in love with his devotion. The character of Sarah is in love with being loved, and The Poet is in love with the Platonic form of love as an ultimate goal. Only

The Jailor seems to have his head screwed on right, and even he is a little too taken with the idea of torture!

There are still problems with the play. I think it's clear from readings that The Poet is a little delusional about Sarah's affections. I think it's clear that there would be no happy ending for them if they were ever to meet again, and so his sacrifice at the end of the play is muted some-what in light of this. Nevertheless, the idea that only one of the characters obeys what he believes to be his true calling, and only one follows devotion to its limit, is inter-esting and worthy of exploration.

The idea as well that to have a vocational calling – be it to God, to love, or to torture – is a desire in us all is inter-esting, and the more I reread the play, the more this takes central precedence for me. The relationship between The Jailor and his Protégé mirrors that of The Poet and The Missionary, and one could believe that if either of them had had someone to show them what The Jailor is showing The Protégé, then neither of them would have ended up in the situation in the first place. Which is, in and of itself, a good enough reason for the play to exist.

Thomas Alexander - Holland 2014

SYNOPSIS

When the lover of a famous writer goes missing in a war ravaged country, he bribes his way into a jail to question her husband, a Missionary who is being tortured as a training exercise for a young trainee jailor.

Alone in the cell the two start a dialogue about the nature of belief. Belief in God, love and politics.

CAST

NOTE: The central cast's ages have been left purposefully vague. There was a sense to the writer that the characters were people in their forties and early fifties but there is no reason to listen to him on this.

THE POET (PETER) Handsome, well dressed.

THE MISSIONARY (SANDY)

SARAH - Attractive and well-dressed but not stylish.

THE JAILOR - Sixties plus. Soft faced. Slim.

THE PROTÉGÉ - Late teens to mid twenties.

PAUL - Twenties. Suited. American.

GUARD - Non speaking part.

VARIOUS VOICES ON TV

Original Concept Sketch
by Thomas Alexander
circ; 2008

© Thomas Alexander 2013

X

THE VISITOR

ACT I

ACT 1

SCENE 1

CURTAINS ON THE OUBLIETTE, A ROUGH PRISON HOLED FROM THE FACE OF A CLIFF, HIGH ABOVE THE COLD LATE AUTUMN LAND BELOW.

THE CELL, CARVED FROM ROCK, HAS A SINGLE DOOR – UPSTAGE – WITH A PEEP-HOLE NEAR THE TOP.

THE ROOM SEEMS TO BE EMPTY. WIND WHISTLES AROUND ITS CRAGGED SPACE GIVING IT AN UNWELCOME AIR. STAGE RIGHT, UNDER A BLANKET - THE SAME SHADE AS THE ROCK FACE - LIES THE PRIEST. HIS BRUISED AND BEATEN BODY, DIRTIED FROM THE OUBLIETTE'S DUST, MAKES HIM INDISTINGUISHABLE FROM THE WALL HE LIES AGAINST, FETAL AGAINST THE COLD.

ABOVE THE SOUND OF THE WIND WE HEAR THE SOUND OF AN OLD CHAIN LIFT, RATCHETING ITS WAY UPWARDS TOWARDS US.

REACHING ITS DESTINATION, IT STOPS AND WE HEAR THE SOUND OF A WROUGHT IRON GATE OPENING.

A PAIR OF FOOTSTEPS – ONE SURE OF ITSELF, THE OTHER NOT – WALK TOWARDS US. THE PEEP-HOLE SLIDES OPEN, REVEALING THE

JAILOR'S FACE. KEYS JANGLE AND THE DOOR OPENS.

THE JAILOR OPENS THE DOOR, A CRACK AT FIRST, AND THEN WIDE. HE STEPS ASIDE LETTING THE POET ENTER, WATCHING HIM CLOSELY AS HE DOES.

THE POET, STRONG AND HANDSOME, ENTERS, UNSURE OF WHAT HE'S LOOKING AT.

FROM HIS PERSPECTIVE THIS IS A CLIFF TOP, A CAVE, NOT A PRISON CELL. HE'S ABOUT TO TURN AND TALK TO THE JAILOR WHEN THE OLDER MAN SHUTS THE DOOR, AND LOCKS IT.

POET   Hey!

THERE IS NO RESPONSE. HE STARTS BANGING ON THE DOOR, AGAIN AND AGAIN, GETTING LOUDER.

POET   Hey! Hey, what is this? Hey!

THE PEEP-HOLE SIDES OPEN, REVEALING THE JAILOR.

POET   What is this? Let me out!

JAILOR   Two days. Then you go. Inspection. Yes?

THE PEEP-HOLE SIDES SHUT.

POET   Hey! HEY!

THE PEEP-HOLE OPENS AGAIN.

JAILOR   Two days. No more!

POET   What is this! Let me out!

THE JAILOR LOOKS AT HIM FOR A MOMENT, THEN SLIDES THE PEEP-HOLE SHUT AGAIN AND OPENS THE DOOR.

JAILOR   You want to go. Go. But deal's deal. There's no change.

POET   What is this? Alessandro Menine. You understand me? You don't get anything until I've seen Alessandro Menine!

AT THE SOUND OF HIS NAME THE MISSION-ARY MOVES, REVEALING HIMSELF TO THE AU-DIENCE. HIS RIGHT EYE IS SWOLLEN SHUT, HIS FACE DIRTY, HIS SKIN MARKED WITH BRUISES.

JAILOR   So see him then!

THE JAILOR GOES ACROSS AND PULLS OFF THE BLANKET. THE PRIEST COWERS BUT THE JAILOR DOES NO MORE, AND RETURNS TO THE DOOR AND THE STARTLED POET.

JAILOR   Two days. No more.

THE JAILOR EXITS, LOCKING THE DOOR BEHIND HIM. WE HEAR THE SOUND OF HIS FOOTSTEPS LEAVING, THE GATE CLOSING, AND THE LIFT DESCENDING ONCE MORE.

THE POET STANDS THERE, STARTLED AT THE SIGHT OF THE MAN, SHOCKED BY WHAT HE'S SEEING AROUND HIM. HE TURNS IN DISBELIEF TO THE DOOR AGAIN.

POET   Hey! What the hell is this?

BUT THE FOOTSTEPS DON'T STOP. THE MISSIONARY, IGNORING THE PRESENCE OF THE POET, PULLS HIMSELF AGAINST THE

WALL, GATHERING HIS STRENGTH. HE CROSS-ES, IGNORING THE POET AS HE HEADS FOR A FOOD CACHE STORED BEHIND A LOOSE ROCK IN THE FISSURE OF THE WALL, BEFORE MOV-ING BACK TO HIS POSITION UNDER THE BLAN-KET.

POET (cont)   Sandy? Alessandro? My god! Sandy. Sandy! It's me. Sandy? It's Peter. Peter Armit-age? You remember? Peter? Sandy? Sandy! Where is she, Sandy? Where is she? Sandy. Where is Sarah, Sandy? Where is she? Sandy! There's no record of her. I've asked everywhere. Did they take her? Sandy? Do they have Sarah? Sandy? Please, Sandy. I prom-ise you! I can help you. I can help her! I just need you to tell me! Sandy? (HE DIGS SOME CHOCOLATE OUT OF HIS BAG) Jesus. Look at you. Sandy? Look. I can help you. Look. I have food. Real food! I think… I can get you out of here Sandy. I can! I can help you. Look, take it. Take it. I can help you, but I need to know. Do they have her? Sandy? Sarah? Do they have her? Is she still in the country? Is she? Sandy? (THE MISSIONARY LOOKS AT THE PROFFERED CHOCOLATE) Yes. Take it. Take it! Really. I can help. I can. Is… Is she still in the country? Sandy? I can help her! (THE MISSIONARY STANDS AGAIN, PUSHING ANGRILY PAST THE POET) Damn it, Sandy! Let me help you!

MISSIONARY   Get away from me!

POET   Sandy!

MISSIONARY   Get away from me!

POET   Sandy. Listen to me. I can help! Just tell me! Tell me! I've… I got access to the prison records. All of them. She's not on any of them. Did they take her, Sandy? Is she still in the country?

MISSIONARY   (QUIETLY) I reject you.

POET   What? Sandy? Sarah, Sandy. Do they have her?

MISSIONARY   (LOUDER) I reject you!

POET   Sandy? Jesus, man, It's me, Peter. Sandy? I can help her, Sandy. I promise I can. I just have to know. Sandy? Do they have her? Is she safe?

THE MISSIONARY TURNS AND WITH VIOLENT STRENGTH THROWS THE POET TO THE GROUND, BEATING HIM WEAKLY WITH HIS FISTS.

MISSIONARY   I reject you! I reject you! You're not real, do you hear me! You're not real!

POET   Jesus, Sandy! What the f…. It's me! Peter!

MISSIONARY   I will not have you here! Understand me! I will not have you here! I will kill you! I will…

THE POET GAINS CONTROL OF THE WEAKENED MAN AND RESTRAINS HIM. THE MISSIONARY STARTS TO CRY.

POET   Get off me! Stop it! Stop it, Sandy! Stop it! I don't want to hurt you but I will if I have to, so just stop. Alright?

MISSIONARY   You're not real.

POET   I am, really. I am. I… I promise.

MISSIONARY   I don't want you here.

POET   I am real. I promise you. Look.
(HE PLACES THE MAN'S HANDS TO HIS FACE) I
am real. Feel me. Feel me. I'm real. I'm really here. I
promise. It's me. Peter.

THE MISSIONARY BREAKS DOWN, TEARS FALL-
ING DOWN HIS FACE AS HE HUGS THE MAN
IN FRONT OF HIM. THE POET, UNCERTAIN AT
FIRST, HUGS BACK.

POET   I'm really here. I promise.

END OF SCENE 1.

SCENE 2

LIGHTS UP ON THE DOWNSTAGE AREA. A HO-
TEL ROOM. LIGHTS FADE ON THE OUBLIETTE

SARAH ENTERS, THROWING HER COAT ONTO
THE BED. SHE IS SOAKED TO THE SKIN.

SARAH   I can't believe you're really here.
(SHE TURNS AND LOOKS BACK AT THE DOOR,
SMILING) Don't be silly. You can come in. Really.
I'm not going to bite.

ENTER THE POET, LIKEWISE SOAKED.

POET   You're sure. I mean…

SARAH   I promise. You (BEAT) might
find a few inappropriate garments strewn around - I
really haven't had time to clean – but I've removed

all the bear traps, promise.

POET   Ha. No it's just, you know. I didn't know if you're... I don't want people to get the wrong impression.

SARAH   Yeah? And what impression would that be? Wet?

POET   You know what I mean.

SARAH   (MOTIONING TO A CHAIR) Put your coat there. You want a towel?

POET   Please.

SARAH   We're old friends. Let them get whatever impression they get. Jesus. I'm soaked through. Here. (SHE TOSSES HIM A TOWEL.) I'm going to change.

EXIT SARAH.

SHE EXITS BUT CONTINUES TALKING OFF-STAGE. THE POET MOVES AROUND THE ROOM LOOKING AT VARIOUS PERSONAL EFFECTS.

SARAH (cont) (OFF) I'd offer you a change of clothes or something but somehow I don't think you'd fit in my dress.

POET   Oh, I don't know.

SARAH (OFF)   I heard that! Anyway, all I've got is summer stuff. So unless you want to go strap-less...

POET   Could be a bold new beginning!

SARAH (OFF)   The transvestite poet? You'd go down a hit in Lower Kensington.

POET   I'm already a hit in Lower Kens-ington. Upper, too!

SARAH (OFF)   What will the drawing rooms of Knightsbridge do with you? You want one of these robes?

POET   Towel's fine.

SARAH (OFF)   Can you believe it? I didn't even bring an umbrella.

POET   That's the problem with these summer countries. You think it's all going to be one heat wave, and suddenly it's Noah's ark out there.

ENTER SARAH.

CHANGED INTO A SUMMER DRESS, THE BACK IS STILL OPEN.

SARAH   Think we should have grabbed some animals on the way in? I saw a couple of rats in the foyer. Here, get this for me, would you?

POET   (ZIPPING HER DRESS.) There're a couple of cockroaches under the bed, but I think they may be hermaphrodites. So we may only need one. Fancy playing god?

SARAH   (TURNING AND IGNORING THE JIBE.) So how long you been here anyway? Please, sit anywhere. You want a drink?

POET   Um. Sure. Coffee?

SARAH   No, I mean a drink!

POET   (SMILING) Oh, I see. Well in that case… Definitely.

SARAH   (FIXING A DRINK) How long you say you've been here?

POET   A week. I've got to tell you. I'm a little... What's the word.

SARAH   Discombobulated?

POET   (TAKING THE DRINK) Thanks. Discombobulated. Exactly.

SARAH   I know what you mean. I saw you in the foyer... This morning? You were coming out of the elevator as I was going in. To breakfast, I suppose. You didn't see me. Or did you?

POET   No, I had no idea.

SARAH   So I've had, like, a few more hours than you to get used to it. But discombobulating. Definitely. Can I do that? Verb the word?

POET   I have absolutely no idea.

SARAH   And there's you, the author.

POET   Poet. Actually.

SARAH   Didn't you write that... thing?

POET   Maker's Mark?

SARAH   (SMILING) I didn't want to...

POET   Remember the title?

SARAH   Inflate your ego.

POET   It's about how you see yourself. Novelists are... I don't know.

SARAH   Unromantic?

POET   Well paid. No. It's just... It helps

you keep things straight, you know what I mean? I'm a poet. A poet who happens to also write a novel or two. It helps keep things in perspective.

SARAH   In that case, can I still do this? May all of your rhymes, fit in their lines, and if they don't, just say fuck it. Cheers.

POET   (LAUGHING) Jesus. Cheers. You know, not every poem in the world has to start with: there was a young man from Nantucket! There is such a thing as free verse.

SARAH   And free towels as well. (MO-TIONING FOR THE TOWEL) Give that here. (MO-TIONING TO THE DRINK) You want another one?

POET   (FINISHING IT QUICKLY) Sure.

SARAH GOES OVER AND STARTS POURING AN-OTHER DRINK.

SARAH   God. I tell you. I really can't believe you're here.

POET   You know, I'm sorry but… I didn't think you could do that.

SARAH   Drink?

POET   Swear.

SARAH   Was I swearing?

POET   God? Taking the Lord's name in vain.

SARAH   Yeah. Bad habit. I probably got that from you. (SHE HANDS HIM HIS DRINK) So what are you doing here? Writing?

10

POET   Lecturing. One of the universities is giving me an honorary degree. You know how it is. They're translating some of my collections into the local language and I'm giving a series of lectures at the campus. It's all embarrassing really.

SARAH   No, it's not!

POET   It is. Really.

SARAH   "The poor man's Ted Hughes."

POET   (LAUGHING) Oh, god. You don't want to take any notice of that! I think my publisher came up with that one.

SARAH   No, I'm proud of you. We all are. We always were.

POET   Well thank you, but really. You don't want to believe everything you read in the press.

SARAH   And you met the queen?

POET   I did. That I did. Meet the queen.

SARAH   She's something, isn't she?

POET   You met the queen?

SARAH   We were doing one of the charity things. You know how it is.

POET   Yeah. And that's what you're doing here now?

SARAH   I am, actually. Yes. You didn't see the posters?

POET   Sorry.

SARAH   Downstairs? In the foyer? We're having a fund-raiser. Tonight. You know I work with the CPA now, right?

POET   I'm sorry, I…

SARAH   Well, I've been working with them for the past few years. Arranging funding, you know, for the schools and - well pretty much everything, really. You've no idea how much it costs.

POET   To run a church?

SARAH   Is that what you think I do? Run a church?

POET   Well, I mean. The missionary's wife…

SARAH   There's… We started this school. An orphanage originally, after the outbreak, but it's pretty much everything now. Boarding school, adult learning centre. And you wouldn't think these things cost a lot of money. You know, not there. I mean it's just wood and books, right? But well, first there's the bribes… Talk about charity! For every pound we want to spend on, you know, important things, we have to spend another two bribing people to let us build it, or stop them from tearing it down. Really. It drives me indiscriminately nuts! I'm not kidding.

POET   People have a very narrow view of who is their own.

SARAH   So, anyway. It costs, all of it. So I work on the money. The CPA do good work, don't spend it all on administration, if you know what I mean. So I help them set up fund-raisers. Things like that. Turns out I'm pretty good at it. Talking people out of their money.

POET   I have no doubt that you are.

PAUSE.

THEY ARE BOTH ASHAMED AT THE GROWING CHEMISTRY BETWEEN THEM.

SARAH   What was it? OBE?

POET   MBE. It's nothing.

SARAH   No. I tell you, if it makes it onto the BBC world service, it's not nothing!

POET   Is that where you heard it?

SARAH   I was cooking.

POET   You used to burn water!

SARAH   I wasn't that bad.

POET   You remember that time, at your parents' place. You insisted on cooking for Jeremy and me, and you made that fried pork?

SARAH   Oh god!

POET   Crispy on the outside, bloody in the middle.

SARAH   Jeremy was sick for a week. He never forgave me.

POET   How is your brother?

SARAH   Good. Good. You know. Something in the city, or whatever they call it these days.

POET   And your husband?

SARAH　　　Sandy.

POET　　　Right.

SARAH　　　He's good. Listen. I'm, you know… There's no easy way to say this. I'm sorry… For not inviting you to the wedding…

POET　　　No, really.

SARAH　　　It was just…

POET　　　No, I understand completely.

SARAH　　　It would have been…

POET　　　We were kids.

SARAH　　　We were.

POET　　　And anyway, I was out of the country.

SARAH　　　Well, there we are then.

POET　　　I couldn't have come anyway.

SARAH　　　Where were you?

POET　　　Paris.

SARAH　　　Really?

POET　　　What?

SARAH　　　We… You were really in Paris?

POET　　　Why not?

SARAH　　　Paris? Not, you know, Paris Texas or something?

POET　　　What's so…

SARAH　　　We were married in Paris.

POET　　　Really?

SARAH   In really Paris. I kid you not.

POET   Huh.

SARAH   You didn't know that?

POET   You never sent me an invite.

SARAH   Point. And you're not…

POET   No. Never.

SARAH   Wow.

POET   What?

SARAH   Well. You say that so absolutely.

POET   Do I?

SARAH   You do.

POET   Yeah, well. (BEAT) He doesn't mind? You travelling so much?

SARAH   He does. Of course he does. But it's for the school, and well….

POET (SHIVERING) Jesus. You know the other problems with places like this?

SARAH   Air conditioning?

POET   You know, I swear to god if they'd invented air-conditioning two hundred years earlier the entire world would be run by the Chinese. The only reason England did so well was that we didn't need siestas. (MOTIONING TO LEAVE) I should…

SARAH   Listen. Come tonight. Are you free?

POET   To the charity thing?

SARAH   Yes, come! Are you free? You should come. Really. You'd love it. Well. OK, that's not true. I usually hate the things, but it'll be a big crowd thing and…

POET   I'm supposed to meet some professors…

SARAH   Blow it off. Or better yet, bring them! Seriously. You'll be a huge hit. Which, in turn, will make me a big hit. Which, in turn, will allow me to relieve them of all their hard earned cash!

POET   I don't know.

SARAH   Please. Come. I don't see many people from, you know, home. And it's too big a co-incidence, us running into each other here.

POET   Serendipity.

SARAH   Divine intervention. I just don't want it to be a five minute thing, you know what I mean? I bump into you. You bump into me. We both get soaked in a rainstorm, and then I never see you again.

POET   How long are you in town? I've got some things I can cancel tomorrow…

SARAH   I'm flying back in the morning.

POET (BEAT)   Then, of course. I'll come. Downstairs?

SARAH   Downstairs. In… (SHE JUMPS UP) God. An hour. I've got to…

POET   You look great. Don't worry.

SARAH   Yeah, right.

POET   I'd better make some calls.

SARAH   Alright.

POET   You want me to come back here or meet you downstairs?

SARAH   Here. We'll go together. What room are you in?

POET   Four-o-two.

SARAH   I'll come to you.

POET   See you in a bit, then. Do you want me to, you know... Read something? I don't know...

SARAH   Just come.

POET   Thank you.

HE MOVES TO EXIT AND THEN TURNS AGAIN.

POET   Sarah. Listen. Not for nothing, but... You look... Fantastic. I just wanted to...

HE EXITS. SARAH WATCHES THE DOOR, THEN SITS, THE SMILE FADING FROM HER FACE.

END OF SCENE 2.

SCENE 3

LIGHTS DOWN ON THE HOTEL ROOM.

LIGHTS UP ON THE OUBLIETTE.

THE POET AND THE MISSIONARY SIT ACROSS

FROM EACH OTHER, LOST IN THOUGHT. THE MISSIONARY IS EATING THE CHOCOLATE.

POET   How long have they kept you like this?

MISSIONARY   I'm... I haven't spoken to any-one in a long time. I'm not used to it.

POET   (STANDING) What is this place?

MISSIONARY   It's an oubliette. A cave. They were... Prisoners... You can jump. It's your choice. You can stay here or you can jump. I think they're waiting for me to...

POET   Why haven't you?

MISSIONARY   (JOKING) Suicide's a sin.

POET   How the hell did you get your-self into this?

MISSIONARY   What's happening? Outside?

POET   There's... I don't know. I don't really watch the news anymore. They finished the election, finally.

MISSIONARY   The country. What's happening with the country?

POET   I'm... You know as much as I do. The border's still closed. They're not talking to the outside world. The rest is... anyone's guess, I suppose. I didn't see anyone else. On the way up. I didn't see anyone else. No corridors. No rooms.

MISSIONARY   At the top of the butte. There's a prison at the top. Twenty or so, I think.

POET   I didn't even know they had buttes.

MISSIONARY   Greek. Originally. Oubliettes.

POET   Well, I like what you've done with the place. Airy.

MISSIONARY   Bijou.

POET   Very... monkish. Birdshit's a nice touch. Pre post-modern, if you know what I mean.

THE MISSIONARY BURSTS INTO A COUGHING FIT.

POET   You must be important to keep you here alone.

MISSIONARY   They think it's... poetic.

POET   And they've kept you here all the time?

MISSIONARY   City. Then they brought me here.

POET   Alone?

MISSIONARY   Alone.

THE MISSIONARY MOVES TO HIDE THE REST OF THE CHOCOLATE.

POET   So that's the choice, is it? Stay here or jump? No, eat it. I have more.

MISSIONARY   Storing. Some days... They stop. Or forget. I can't tell which. I... I thought you were a ghost. I thought... I thought perhaps I'd gone mad, you know. I kept thinking I would. I kept... I talked to things. At first. I sang. Birds come in here sometimes. Crows. Checking… I talked to them at first. It was… ironic. I think. I was a man worried about madness, but I thought maybe I was going mad. I was losing… So I stopped. I stopped talking to them. The birds. And I thought, perhaps you were because of that. I thought because I'd stopped talking…

POET   Where is she?

MISSIONARY   I thought, of all the things that I could create, of all the people… You… Do you understand?

POET   Where is she?

MISSIONARY   See, God… If this is all some kind of test. From God? Well, God I can handle. God has a purpose, but my mind… You understand.

POET   Is she still in the country?

MISSIONARY   What happened to Navratil?

POET   They shot him.

MISSIONARY   Really.

POET   In the square. And in the head. In that order. Couldn't have happened to a nicer guy.

MISSIONARY   You ever seen anyone shot?

POET   No.

MISSIONARY   Then you don't know what the hell you're talking about.

POET   I… bribed. I bribed a lot of people. Revolution is a costly business it seems. There was this man, in the central bureau. That's what they're calling it now. Bureau au Politic. He got me a list of foreigners who were being held. Your name was on it. With this address. I don't know any more than that. You're costing me a fortune.

MISSIONARY   You're not doing it for me.

POET   No.

MISSIONARY   When did…?

POET   I see her?

MISSIONARY   The last time.

POET   (PAUSE) I heard from her about eight months ago. A phone call. She was fading in and out. It was already underway by then. She said you were getting out of the country. Both of you. I figured it was just a question of waiting. So I waited. Four months ago the CPA contacted me, asking if I'd heard from her. I got in touch with the consulate but… There was no record of you crossing the border. Not that that was terribly unusual. I spoke with your church…

MISSIONARY   You spoke with the church?

POET   For all the good it did me. Turn the other cheek seems to be the motto when dealing with warlords and dictators. Finally I spoke with a camera crew. American. They told me they'd helped you. Been working with you at the… Well, mission, they called it. Before the uprising.

MISSIONARY   Did they mention anything about a boy? Kinhio?

POET   I… I wouldn't have known to ask.

THIS HAS A GREAT EFFECT ON THE MISSION-
ARY.

POET   (cont) The one thing I couldn't
find any record of… was her.

MISSIONARY   You can get me out of here?

POET   Maybe. I think so. Not from
here. I mean, these guys are as greedy as the next
guy, but the jailors here aren't going to just let you
out. No matter what the price. They'd be killed. The
new regime… I can get you out. I know I can. But I
need to be on the outside. Now we know where you
are…

MISSIONARY   You can smell things, sometimes. On the wind. You can smell… Cooking? They
had a bag on my head when I came here. Is there a
camp at the bottom?

POET   There's a house. A guard's
house, I guess. There's a chimney.

MISSIONARY   I'd never thought of it.

POET   What?

MISSIONARY   Are they married, do you think?
I never really thought about it before. Is there a wife
at the bottom of the cliff, cooking supper for them?

POET   I wouldn't know.

MISSIONARY   It's… I've never thought of
them outside the context of… this.

POET   Why the hell were you doing to
them? Proselytizing….

MISSIONARY   (LAUGHING) Proselytizing ,

yes. That was it! It doesn't matter.

POET   What did you mean before?
Loved her.

MISSIONARY   The boy? The one I mentioned
before. He was with me when I was arrested. We
were… We were driving back into the city. It's… We
think fighting starts in the cities, don't we. Usually
not. (BEAT) We never even made in back into the
centre.

POET   I can help you. I can. From the
outside. But Sandy…. If she's in prison. If she's being
held. Whatever you think of me. I can help her. I can.
You just have to tell me. You just have to…

MISSIONARY   (VENOMOUSLY) You use…
You use emotions like words. Like I use words.

POET   Does it matter? If she's safe,
does any of it matter?

MISSIONARY   It's sickening. How long were
you lying with my wife?

THE POET LAUGHS.

MISSIONARY (cont)What?

POET   No. Lying? Lying? Is that what
they teach you in… I'm sorry. It's just…

MISSIONARY   Six years? Give or take?

POET   None of that matters…

MISSIONARY   It matters! Of course it matters!
It matters to me. You really expect me to help you?
You?

POET   I expect you to help her! Whatever you thought of her, she was with you! She was
your responsibility! Yours! Jesus, man. Let me help
you! Let me help her. What…?

THE SOUND OF THE LIFT CHAIN ASCENDING
STARTS. THE MISSIONARY RISES, MOVING TO
THE EDGE.

MISSIONARY   They're coming.

POET   What do you…?

MISSIONARY   I… Leave me alone.

POET   Jesus. Move away from the
edge!

MISSIONARY   Leave me alone!

POET   Don't be stupid. They're probably just going up!

THE LIFT CRANK STOPS AND WE HEAR THE
DOOR SLIDE OPEN. THE MISSIONARY   RE-
TURNS TO HIS PLACE.

MISSIONARY   No no no no no no no.

POET   What..? Sandy? Sandy?

THE PEEP-HOLE SLIDES BACK AND THE PRO-
TÉGÉ LOOKS IN. IT SLIDES SHUT AGAIN AND
THE DOOR OPENS.

POET   Hey, can we get some help in
here?

ENTER JAILOR AND PROTÉGÉ.

THE PROTÉGÉ IS ARMED.

JAILOR   (TO THE POET) Sit over there.

POET   What's…

THE PROTÉGÉ STEPS UP AND POINTS THE GUN
DIRECTLY AT THE POET'S HEAD.

PROTÉGÉ   He said get over here!

POET   (MOVING AWAY) Jesus! Fine.
Fine. Whatever. Just… Get that thing out of my face!

JAILOR   You get what you want?

POET   What? No! I…

PROTÉGÉ   Should maybe have talked fast-
er.

JAILOR   (TO PROTÉGÉ) Get his arms.

THE PAIR PULL AT THE ARMS OF THE SITTING
MISSIONARY WHO WHIMPERS BUT DOESN'T
RESIST.

POET   Where are you taking him?

JAILOR   You want to go?

POET   I have two days! You said two
days!

PROTÉGÉ   Stay where you fucking are,
man. I mean it!

THE PAIR BEGIN TO DRAG THE MISSIONARY
OUT OF THE ROOM. THE POET STAYS ROOTED
TO HIS CORNER.

POET   Sandy! Sandy! Where are you
taking him? Sandy!

SUDDENLY HE JUMPS UP IN FRONT OF THEM.

POET   This is ridiculous!

PROTÉGÉ   Get the fuck back!

POET   (TO SANDY) Where is she! Tell me! For god's sake!

MISSIONARY   Dead.

THE PROTÉGÉ PUSHES THE POET BACK TO THE FLOOR AND THE THREE EXIT, DRAGGING THE MISSIONARY BETWEEN THEM. THE DOOR SLAMS SHUT LEAVING THE POET ALONE IN THE CELL.

END OF SCENE 3.

SCENE 4

LIGHTS UP ON THE BEDROOM. SARAH IS ALONE IN THE BED, SLEEPY. SHE WAKES, CHECKS THE CLOCK, THEN PULLS THE COVERS OVER HER HEAD AGAIN.

THE LIGHTS FADE ON THE OUBLIETTE.

ENTER POET.

HE COMES IN QUIETLY, THE LIGHTS HALF ON, AND SITS GENTLY ON THE SIDE OF THE BED WATCHING SARAH SLEEP.

SHE STIRS, SEES HIM THERE, TURNS AND SITS UP RUBBING HER EYES.

SARAH   You scared me.

POET   Sorry.

SARAH   I was asleep.

POET   Sorry.

SARAH   You just getting in?

POET   Yeah, I'm sorry. My... The flight was delayed. I tried to use one of those phones they've got there, but I didn't know the hotel number and...

SARAH   I was asleep.

POET   Yeah. Come here.

THEY HUG.

SARAH   I must look terrible.

POET   Well...

SARAH   I was asleep!

POET   So you keep saying.

HE KISSES HER PASSIONATELY BUT SHE PULLS AWAY.

SARAH   I'm... Oh, god, what time is it?

POET   Four.

SARAH   I was dreaming. I... How did you get in here?

POET   Stanzas.

SARAH   I'm sorry?

POET   The girl at the front desk. I wrote four stanzas on the Dubai experience. (BEAT) I'm kidding. The room's in my name remember? Go back to sleep. I'll take the couch and...

SARAH   No, I'm up. I'm up. I'm… I'm sorry. It's… It's wonderful to see you again. It's just…

POET   I know. Don't worry about it.

SARAH   I'm not used to this.

POET   Me too. How's the charity?

SARAH   CPS?

POET   It's CPS now?

SARAH   Yeah. Ridiculous, isn't it. You know what the problem is? Money. You want coffee? (HE SIGNALS NO) These things all start out with the best of intentions, you know, and they… (SHE YAWNS) They start out with the best of intentions and then they make money. And suddenly, you know, it's a full time job, so you've got to pay someone and it grows and suddenly there's logistics and it's too big for one person and before you know it half the money you're making is being spent on administration. And suddenly it's not a charity anymore, not really. It's an organization. You know? And you start to wonder, don't you? Is it really worth giving money to these people so they can keep driving… Whatever they're driving. It's ridiculous.

POET   I can't stand the fact that all men start out with the idea of Madonna and end with the reality of Sodom.

SARAH   That you?

POET   Dostoevsky. Basically.

SARAH   Big on pop singers, was he?

POET   What's the solution?

SARAH   I have no idea. The little charities. They do good, but they can't reach the places the big ones can so…

POET   You keep reinventing yourselves.

SARAH   If the governments…

POET   Oh, god. Politics at dawn. Very sexy!

SARAH   I know. I'm sorry. Not the kind of thing you really want to hear, is it.

POET   No, it's… fine. Really. This is part of who you are and … I want to hear about you.

SARAH   Not exactly Last Tango in Paris, is it?

POET   Oh, sweetheart! I've been on a plane for eighteen hours. You start a tango and it's going to aggravate my deep vein thrombosis.

SARAH   I was having the strangest of dreams.

POET   Come here.

SARAH LAUGHS GIRLISHLY AND CRAWLS ACROSS THE BED TOWARDS HIM. THEY KISS, BECOMING PASSIONATE, AND FALL BENEATH THE COVERS.

THEY BREAK. SARAH SNUGGLES INTO HIM.

SARAH   I missed you.

POET   I always miss you.

SARAH   (SUDDENLY AWAKE) What

time's your thing in the morning?

POET   I'm not even sure what morning it is!

SARAH   I set the alarm for eight.

POET   I'm still on LA time.

SARAH   …'m fading.

POET   I know.

SARAH   Can you sleep?

POET   As soon as my brain passes the Christmas Islands. Don't worry about it.

SARAH   'Kay. I really missed you.

POET   Go to sleep.

HE SITS THERE FOR A MINUTE WATCHING HER, THEN UNTANGLES HIMSELF AND STANDS SLOWLY, MOVING AWAY FROM THE BED.

LIGHTS FADE ON THE BED.

END OF SCENE 4.

SCENE 5

LIGHTS UP ON THE OUBLIETTE.

THE POET IS ALONE IN THE ROOM, WAITING AND REMEMBERING, HIS MANNER ANXIOUS AND CONFUSED.

WE HEAR THE SOUND OF THE ELEVATOR,

RATCHETING DOWN TOWARDS US.

THE POET RISES AND LOOKS AT THE DOOR. WE HEAR THE STEEL GATE PULLED BACK AND FOOTSTEPS COMING TOWARDS US.

THE POET PACES.

THE DOOR OPENS AND THE THREE RE-ENTER, DRAGGING A BARELY CONSCIOUS AND CLEARLY TORTURED MISSIONARY. THE JAILOR AND THE PROTÉGÉ KEEP THEIR EYES ON THE POET AS THEY DEPOSIT HIM ON THE OTHER SIDE OF THE OUBLIETTE.

JAILOR   (TO POET) Do you have anything to say? About your friend? Nothing?

POET   He's not my friend.

THE JAILOR NODS AND TURNS AWAY. THE PROTÉGÉ FINISHES DUMPING THE BODY.

JAILOR   (TO PROTÉGÉ) Come.

THE TWO MEN LEAVE. THE PROTÉGÉ MAKES A THREATENING GESTURE TO THE POET AND IS PLEASED WHEN HE FLINCHES.

THE POET WAITS UNTIL THE TWO MEN LEAVE AND THEN HURRIES OVER TO THE PRONE BODY, SHOCKED AT WHAT HAPPENING BUT RESOLUTE.

POET   Jesus! Sandy? Sandy?

MISSIONARY   Cold.

THE POET MOVES HIM, COVERING HIM WITH BOTH THE BLANKET AND HIS OWN COAT. HE SHIVERS IN THE WIND. THE MISSIONARY

WATCHES HIM BLANKLY.

POET   Where is she? Sandy? Where is she! Do you hear me? Sandy? Damn it man, they're… You've got to tell me where she is! I can hel…

MISSIONARY   I told you. She's dead.

THE POET SITS BACK.

POET   Bullshit.

MISSIONARY   You don't believe me?

POET   If she was dead I'd know.

MISSIONARY   Fire. They set her on fire. All of them. It wasn't personal. It was a matter of expediency, nothing more. Women burn white. You know that? Fat content. Men burn orange but women burn white.

POET   You're lying.

MISSIONARY   Simpler than arresting them. Simpler than waiting them out. They simply burnt the building down.

POET   Stop it.

MISSIONARY   They took them out of the church and shot her in the head.

POET   Before or after they burnt them alive?

MISSIONARY   She contracted aids. A bad needle, nothing more.

POET   It's not funny.

MISSIONARY   (LIFTING HIS SHIRT PAIN-

FULLY) Tomorrow I'll bleed painfully from places you never want to see blood come out, so why don't you let me be the judge of what's funny or not.

THE TWO ARE SILENT FOR A FEW MINUTES.

POET   What the hell did you do to them?

MISSIONARY   (LAUGHING) I did nothing to them! I did nothing to anybody!

POET   You… Why did you bring her here? You knew it was dangerous! After Zambia? How could you have made her come here with you!

MISSIONARY   I couldn't make her do anything, and she didn't come here for me.

POET   Of course she came here for you. For your stupid religion…

MISSIONARY   You don't know what you're talking about.

POET   For your crusade! She came here because you told her to come.

MISSIONARY   No.

POET   She came here because you told her it was the worst place in the world, because you told her it was where she was needed the most!

MISSIONARY   You're wrong.

POET   She was a sucker for a bleeding heart and you told her to come here.

MISSIONARY   She came here to escape you! (PAUSE) You know nothing about her. Nothing.

You think saying something and meaning it is the same thing. It's not! You think you loved her. Is that it? You think… You are such a fool. You knew nothing about her. Nothing. (PAUSE) You… It was her idea to come here. Did you know that? After Zambia? It was her idea! I wanted to take her home. I was offered a church. A… I wanted her to be near family. Friends. You, even. I… She chose to come here. She spoke to the deacons… She wanted to get away from you.

POET   You were working with the FRJ. Is that why?

MISSIONARY   You don't know what you're talking about.

POET   The FR…

MISSIONARY   What is that? Is that a name you read in the newspapers? Is that what that is? FRJ? There was no rebellion! There were no rebels! It's… It's got to be a story, doesn't it? The world. It has to fit into neat little narratives? This side or that. Is that it? Companies evil, governments good. Governments evil, rebels good. Is that what it is? It doesn't work like that. People are mean and stupid. People are mean and stupid and God loves them. That's all there is. There are no rebels.   There are no struggling masses. People hurt people. There's no organization about it. There doesn't have to be. FRJ? I never met anyone from any group calling themselves FRJ, yet the world thinks that every teenager with a gun is that.

POET   The FRJ are the people who helped me get in here.

MISSIONARY   No, they weren't. People pick up a name. They need a banner. FRJ, IRA, al Qaeda – they're as good as any. People pick up names.

POET   Which one was she working with?

MISSIONARY   Let me sleep.

POET   What the hell is it with people and countries. I get... I can understand the idea of fighting for something you believe in. I can understand wanting to pick up arms and right an injustice. But a country? Land. Stupid antiquated notions that mean nothing. (BEAT) One person at a time.

MISSIONARY   (PAUSE) When I came here, I don't know.... There were... They'd closed the churches. All of them. It didn't matter what denomination. It didn't matter what anyone believed. You believed in the country or you believed in nothing. You know what a country is? It's what you know. What you know! The food you eat. The way you talk. Sports. Language. That's all it is. A country. When I came here... When we came here. It was stupid, that's what it was. You hear, you hear about landmines aimed at children, you know, toys... And you hear about roadside bombs, indiscriminate. You hear about all this but you don't hear what living with this kind of life does to people. What it... People hate each other. There's no trust, and when there's no trust there's fear and anger and...

PAUSE

POET   She told me you were coming here with the mission.

THE MISSIONARY NODS.

POET (cont)   She kept changing charities… I mean. It wasn't enough… (HE SMILES) She used to complain, did you know that? All the time. She used to complain about each of them. Each one. She'd join a new charity like they were the second c o m i n g and then six months later she'd be all over them. Hating them.

MISSIONARY   I had to stop her giving away everything we had.

POET   Were you in the capital during the coup?

MISSIONARY   Just outside it. We heard it though. Heard it all the way down the road. That's another thing that changes. In… We're used to hearing it on the TV, you know? I was in London during the bombing. (PAUSE) We both were. First thing we did was turn on the TV. Turn on the TV to find out what's happening outside our door. Here it's rumour. It's whatever someone tells you. That's what you tell other people. And soon everyone believes the same thing. Or different things. And that becomes the truth. Boy robs a store – it's the FRJ. A family are killed in their home – it's the government. Doesn't matter if it's true. It's part of what it is.

POET   What do they want from you?

MISSIONARY   You think you know her, but you don't. You get to meet people. Good people, bad people. Same people you want to bring medicine in, bring guns. Same people. Humanitarianism and inhumanity go hand in hand. You want to get things done in... You've got to... Corrupt people are corrupt on all levels. Guns, secrets, medicine. It's all the same. You're shipping one, you're shipping them all. You know nothing about her.

WE HEAR THE SOUND OF THE ELEVATOR COMING UP. THE MISSIONARY WINCES AND PULLS THE COVERS OVER HIM.

POET   People cause their own misery. Why get involved?

THE PEEP-HOLE SLIDES BACK.

POET (cont)   For god's sake man, just tell them! If there's something you know, tell them! It can't do them any good now!

THE MISSIONARY IS SILENT.

THE POET GOES UP TO THE DOOR, ANXIOUS AGAIN. THE PEEP-HOLE SLIDES OPEN AND THE PROTÉGÉ LOOKS IN.

POET   This wasn't part of the deal!

PROTÉGÉ   Step back.

POET   He's no good...

PROTÉGÉ   Step back!

THE POET STEPS BACK AND THE DOOR OPENS.

THE PROTÉGÉ ENTERS CARRYING A TRAY WITH TWO BOWLS OF GRUEL.

PROTÉGÉ   Room service!

POET   This wasn't part of the deal. He's no good to me dead! Two days!

THE PROTÉGÉ IGNORES HIM AND MOVES ACROSS TO THE MISSIONARY, WHO STAYS PRONE ON THE FLOOR.

THE PROTÉGÉ KICKS HIM.

PROTÉGÉ   Still with us, Father? Yeah, you're still here, aren't you, shithead. Soup time!

POET   He needs medical attention!

PROTÉGÉ   Yeah? Need medical help, do you Father? (HE KICKS HIM AGAIN) Want me to take you back upstairs? Put a little band aid on it for you, Father?

POET   Stop it. He's not Catholic!

PROTÉGÉ   See, he doesn't need a hospital, do you Father? No. See. He's fine! Isn't that right, Father?

POET   I get two days. That's the deal!

PROTÉGÉ   (GIVING HIM THE BOWL OF GRUEL) You get what I give you. Ain't that right, Father? Yeah. You get what I give.

POET   There's to be no more torture! Not while I'm here. Tell your boss that!

THE PROTÉGÉ TURNS, HIS DEMEANOUR CHANGING.

PROTÉGÉ   Listen. You a writer then, are you?

POET   Why?

PROTÉGÉ   How do you get into that, then? You need schooling?

POET   I don't know. Not really.

PROTÉGÉ   What kind of thing you write?

POET   I'm... I'm a poet. Mainly. A couple of novels.

PROTÉGÉ   TV?

POET   No. That's... It's a different medium.

PROTÉGÉ   Yeah. (BEAT) You like my English?

POET   I don't...

PROTÉGÉ   I learnt it off TV. Good yeah? How'd you get into writing TV?

POET   I... I wouldn't know.

PROTÉGÉ   Not much of a writer then, are you? Two days. Room and board. Nothing more. And we do to him what we like. Be thankful we don't do to you.

HE TURNS TO GO AND THEN TURNS BACK.

PROTÉGÉ (cont) Forgot to bless the soup.

HE SPITS INTO THE POET'S BOWL, TURNS, AND AS AN AFTERTHOUGHT KICKS OVER THE BOWL.

PROTÉGÉ (cont) See you tomorrow, Father!

THE PROTÉGÉ EXITS.

WE HEAR THE SOUND OF FOOTSTEPS, THE DOOR, AND THE ELEVATOR DESCENDING. THE MISSIONARY TRIES TO GATHER THE LAST

OF THE BROTH ON THE FLOOR.

POET   What on earth can it matter? Now. For god's sake, just tell them what they want to know. Everyone's probably either dead or gone anyway.

MISSIONARY   (LOOKING UP) Now, yes. I told them everything on the first day. In the first ten minutes.

END OF SCENE 5.

SCENE 6

LIGHTS DOWN ON THE OUBLIETTE. LIGHTS UP ON THE BEDROOM.

SARAH IS SITTING ON THE BED, AN ANGER SUBSIDING IN HER.

THERE IS A KNOCKING AT THE DOOR. SARAH IGNORES IT.

A PAUSE, THEN THE KNOCKING INCREASES.

POET (OFF)   Sarah! Open the door!

SHE CONTINUES TO IGNORE IT, THE ANGER GROWING ONCE MORE. SHE PULLS A SUIT-CASE FROM UNDER THE BED AND BEGINS TO PACK.

POET (cont OFF)   Sarah! Dammit! Stop being such

a child! The room's in my name, for Christ's sake. You want me to go back down to the desk and get another key?

SHE STALKS ACROSS AND OPENS THE DOOR, BEFORE RETURNING TO THE BED ONCE MORE.

POET   You're leaving? Great. That's just great. One fucking fight and you leave me. Him…

SARAH   Oh, grow up! It's not… This is stupid. I don't want to have this argument!

POET   So much so that you'll throw us in rather than deal with what's really going on here!

SARAH   What's…? Oh, that's rich! What's going on is I'm leaving.

POET   (CLOSING THE BAG ON HER ANGRILY) No, you're not. You're staying here and we're going to deal with it! It's been three days, Sarah. Three days! Three days and you decide you can't live with me? It usually takes women the better part of six months to learn they can't live with me!

SARAH   Is that supposed to be funny?

POET   I didn't…

SARAH   Great. Six months. I'm a fast learner. This was a mistake. Is that what you want to hear? This is a mistake!

POET   Sarah…

SARAH   And I'm not just talking about this. All of this. It was a mistake. I don't know what I was thinking. Jesus. I must have been crazy.

POET   Can you just… Just stop. For a minute. I'll call you a cab if you like. I'll do it myself. There's not going to be any flights at this time anyway but… Please stop. For a minute.

SARAH   I wanted romance. Just a little romance, you know? I'm… That's all I wanted, alright? Just romance. To feel… All this… I'm married. Married. You understand that? Married! And I love my husband. Really. He is twice the man you are. On his worst day he is twice the man you are! This… I wanted a bit of romance. That's all! To feel… wanted! I should never have… It didn't mean anything, you understand? It…

POET   Stop. Just… Stop. I didn't hear anything after married.

SARAH   Why did you… What made you think…

POET   Just…

SARAH   It was a sin. I knew it. A sin

POET   Oh, bullshit!

SARAH   It was. A sin! A sin against God. Against my husband…

POET   Bullshit! Bullshit! You want to… You want to pretend this was just… something? Go ahead! You want to make like it didn't mean anything to you, fine. But don't bring your bullshit religion into it! This has nothing to do with God. Nothing!

SARAH   It was a sin! You can't even understand that. I was, Jesus, I am, cheating. It doesn't matter what you believe. It's a sin!

POET   You think this is good for me? You think this is easy?

SARAH   Fucking another man's wife? Yeah, it's really hard!

POET   (VIOLENTLY ANGRY) Do not...! Do not call it that. I've fucked. I've fucked a lot of times...

SARAH   I'm sure you have.

POET   This was not fucking. It wasn't! If there was ever a definition of making love it's what we have. Leave your fucking God out of it! You want to leave, leave, but do not – do not – belittle what's between us.

SARAH   You can't stand it, can you? People with faith? All your talk of beauty and existentialism but you can't even extend that far, can you.

POET   I have no problem with people believing...

SARAH   You can't stand it! There is a God! I believe that! There is a God and he watches and judges...

POET   Jesus.

SARAH   And he judges. Me! He judges me! When I'm with you, he judges me!

POET   Do you even listen to yourself?

SARAH   You will never understand our faith.

POET   Our faith?

SARAH   Yes. Our faith! What, did you think I didn't believe as well? Did you think I was just a missionary's heathen wife?

POET   I believe. I have faith! I have faith in people and…

SARAH   Jesus!

POET   I have faith in people and ideas and community…

SARAH   Words! All of it. You have faith in words! You talk and talk but it's all just words. What do you do? Nothing? You do nothing! You write words and you think that makes you an expert? On people? On faith? You think that makes you an expert on what anyone but you thinks?

POET   You know what I think? I think you can't walk away so you're burning it all down. That's what I think. (SILENCE) I think you saw something tonight that frightened you. Something that…

SARAH   (SOFTER) What am I doing here, Peter? What…. This dress? Those people…

POET   It was an award dinner…

SARAH   And that's your life, isn't it. What did you call it?

POET   (JOKING) Epicurean?

SARAH   Those people. Those terrible, terrible people. I…

POET   They're just people. You deal

with people like that all the time! The charity…

SARAH   I'm on the other side from them. I… They're… I don't talk to them, not like that. I don't. We talk about the charity. I didn't… What purpose did I have? What reason? What reason did you have? I was watching you up there on the podium and I just kept thinking how stupid it all was. All of it! How pointless. And you, with your words, with all those beautiful words, how pointless you seemed to me. How stupidly pointless.

POET   I'm sorry to hear that.

SARAH   And there it is! First time tonight. I've finally hurt you, haven't I?

POET   Have you ever stopped to think? Have you ever… An area is starving. People are dying. You go in there with medicine and food and keep them alive. You keep them… They're dependent on you! They're dependent! The area couldn't support that many people in the first place and you just gave them a life, a life to have kids, which you'll also keep alive. And now there're too many people in the region and they're dependant on you. Totally dependent. All the irrigation in the world isn't going to keep that many people alive in an area like that, and no one likes being dependent, so they… They grow up. They grow up and fight. Each other. You. They breed and kill and hate because that's the only thing they can, other than wait for you to put more rice on their table. You don't move them to another area which can support them. You can't! The people living there won't let you, and you can't bring them back to civilization. There's too many of them!

SARAH   You don't know what you're talking about.

POET   Don't I? Have you ever stopped to think…

SARAH   Fuck you. Civilization? Fuck yourself!

POET   Alright…

SARAH   You help the ones in front of you. You help the ones that need help. It isn't about them. You can't even see that! It's about you. You!

POET   That's just a little selfish, isn't it.

SARAH   Selfish is thinking that just because other people might cause more problems for you, you should let them die.

POET   Alright. I didn't mean that.

SARAH   It won't work. Can't you see that?

POET   You're talking about us?

SARAH   We're different worlds. Completely different.

POET   I know this. Walking out now… Walking out won't make it work. I… I love you. I know you think that's easy for me to say and everything, but it's not. You go home every time to him and it hurts. But I stay alive because I know, in reality, you love me too. I know… Tonight was a mistake. I'm sorry. It was a mistake. You've given him eight years. Give me one week. That's all I'm asking.

SARAH   We have, anyway.

POET   What?

SARAH   Six months. You said it took women six months to know they couldn't live with you. We met again six months ago. Tomorrow.

POET   It was just a stupid line.

SARAH   Isn't that what they always are? Lines? Goodbye Peter.

EXIT SARAH.

FADE TO BLACK.

END OF SCENE 6.

SCENE 7

LIGHTS DOWN ON THE BEDROOM.

IT'S SUNSET IN THE OUBLIETTE. THE LAST VESTIGES OF THE SUN ARE FALLING OUT OF THE ROOM, SHROUDING IT IN DARKNESS.

THE MISSIONARY IS SITTING IN HIS CUSTOMARY POSITION RESTING AND WATCHING THE POET AS HE WRITES SOMETHING ON A PIECE OF PAPER GLEANED FROM HIS BAG.

MISSIONARY   It's beautiful, isn't it?

THE POET LOOKS UP.

MISSIONARY (cont)Horror from beauty.

POET   (LOOKING OUT TO THE HO-RIZON) Is that Kardisn? To the left over there?

MISSIONARY   When does it happen, do you think? At some point… People move from wanting to be left alone, to… One minute you're a family, thinking about work and… dinner and… and grand-children, and the next you're a mob, walking down the street, intent on killing some group of people you don't even know. How do they go back to it, do you wonder? Doesn't it seem… false. (PAUSE) What are you writing?

POET   Something. I'm not sure yet.

MISSIONARY   There's this thing… A myth. The Lords of Shouting. Beautiful, really. They… Every morning ten million angels sing to God as he pushes the sun up into the sky. Beautiful. And I've often wondered… What happens at sunset?

POET   That's Jewish, isn't it?

MISSIONARY   Kabbalah, I think..

POET   I didn't think you'd care about Jewish mysticism.

MISSIONARY   Comparative religion. Second year of university. (PAUSE) Can I read it?

POET   Perhaps. When it's finished. The light's gone now. It's too dark. (PAUSE) Anyway, it is sunrise, right?

MISSIONARY   What do you mean?

POET   Somewhere. If the sun's going down here, somewhere…

MISSIONARY   I'd never thought of it like that.

POET   It means the Lords must always be shouting.

MISSIONARY   Maybe there're different ones. For each country.

POET   Maybe it's only over Zion.

MISSIONARY   Somehow I doubt that.

THE SUNLIGHT HAS ALL FADED.

A SMALL PATCH OF MOONLIGHT ILLUMI-NATES THE FRONT OF THE OUBLIETTE, DIPPING OVER THE CLIFF INTO THE CAVE BEYOND. THE MAJORITY IS, HOWEVER, COMPLETELY BLACK.

MISSIONARY   She was eighteen when I met her. Did she tell you that? You didn't come to the wedding. She'd mentioned you, of course. I'd never heard of you. Even when you became famous, I didn't hear of you. Except from her.

POET   I know all this.

MISSIONARY   We met at a seminar on Mat-thew – the gospel. The Kingdom of Heaven I think it was. She was only eighteen, but bright... You know her father was a preacher, I suppose. One of those lay preachers. The kind that stand behind a wooden pul-pit and bark out the fear of damnation. Why weren't you at the wedding?

THE POET LIGHTS A CIGARETTE IN HIS COR-NER OF THE OUBLIETTE, IT LIGHTING HIM FOR A MOMENT.

POET   I was out of the country. Cigarette?

MISSIONARY   I don't smoke.

THE POET LAUGHS AND THROWS THE PACKET WITHIN REACH OF THE MISSIONARY. A LIGHTER FOLLOWS. THERE'S SILENCE AS THE MISSIONARY LIGHTS ONE AND COUGHS AT HIS FIRST SMOKE.

POET   I met her first when I was, what was it, eight? Ten? I don't remember. My friend was in love with her. We had a house in her town and we used to spend the summer there. He was a local boy. Kept telling me about her. I saw her through a window in the back of her father's car. Nothing more than that. She never mentioned you. At the college.

MISSIONARY   She used to argue with the lecturers. Always arguing. The Eucharist, Augustine... I don't think there was anything she didn't disagree with.

POET   It was her father's idea. University. She told me she'd made a pact with him. A degree in theology and he'd let her go her own way. It was her way of being...   Such a useless thing. Religion.

MISSIONARY   Like poetry.

POET   Poetry doesn't start wars.

MISSIONARY   Then what's the importance of it? (PAUSE) How do you do that, anyway?

POET   What?

MISSIONARY   Become a poet.

POET   How do you become a missionary?

MISSIONARY   Is there a job application or something? Or do you just decide you're going to do it? How… Who buys poetry? Seriously. How on earth can you make a living writing poetry?

POET   A strong knowledge of verbs.

MISSIONARY   And yet your… How many houses do you have? It must be nice coming from privilege.

POET   Yeah, listen. I'm not about to compare what we do or anything, but I work hard for what I get. I spend six months of the year travelling…

MISSIONARY   Listen to yourself! You go around the world collecting platitudes from people who don't know any better. And for what? What was that last one?

POET   Euripides. It was a collection about Euripides.

MISSIONARY   (LAUGHING) Well, that's just classic isn't it. Yes. Way to give back something to the world with that one.

POET   It's not like you're employable in any other part of the world, is it? I mean, missionary? Really? In this day and age? Have you ever noticed that people who work in churches are the kind of people who could only get a job writing articles for a local newspaper? Wanted, saving the world through Jesus. Must be articulate, irrational, and able to obstinately adhere to a set of doctrines that would make Pol Pot look like a humanitarian. What on earth makes you think there's a God?

THE POET'S CIGARETTE DIES DOWN AND HE STUBS IT OUT.

MISSIONARY   Not in here. Throw it over the cliff. If you throw it in here they'll notice.

THE POET STANDS AND MAKES HIS WAY TO THE MOONLIT EDGE.

POET   I just don't understand how someone with… Someone who's seen as much as you have can believe in God? The Christian God. How do you reconcile it? How do you… keep believing?

HE TOSSES THE BUTT OVER THE EDGE OF THE CLIFF.

POET   (cont) Jesus, it's cold. If winter…

THE MISSIONARY COMES AT HIM OUT OF THE DARK, DRIVING HIM TOWARDS THE EDGE, HOPING TO THROW HIM OVER. THE TWO MEN HIT THE FLOOR INCHES FROM THE EDGE, THE MISSIONARY ON TOP.

MISSIONARY   (SCREAMING) I am your God! I am your God! You have worshipped at my table! You have worshipped at my table!

THE POET THROWS THE WEAKENED MAN OFF AND THE TWO STARE AT EACH OTHER ACROSS THE MOONLIGHT.

POET   Get off me! Get off me! What are

you, crazy? You could have killed us both!

MISSIONARY   She was my wife!

POET   You could have killed us!

MISSIONARY   She was my wife! My wife!

HE BEGINS TO CRY.

THE MISSIONARY HAS BEEN SCRATCHED IN THE FIGHT AND HE CHECKS   HIMSELF FOR BLOOD, HOLDING HIS HAND UP TO THE MOONLIGHT.

POET   Jesus! (PURPOSEFULLY) Jesus! You could have killed us both!

MISSIONARY   (LAUGHING) I should stay alive so my wife's lover can come by for visits? Should I expect poems? Cigarettes? This is supposed to mean something to me?

POET   I'm the only thing keeping you alive and you know it!

MISSIONARY   (CRAWLING BACK INTO THE DARK) What makes you think I want to live? Get out   of here. Just... Get out.

POET   Where is she buried?

MISSIONARY   No.

POET   She's alive, isn't she?

MISSIONARY   No more stories. Go.

POET   I'm not leaving until you tell me.

SILENCE

MISSIONARY   Pray there's a God. Pray to him.
I swear. Pray to him they kill me because I promise, I
will kill you. If you stay here I will kill you. Pray for
that!

POET   How did she die?

FADE TO BLACK.

END OF ACT I.

THE VISITOR

ACT II

ACT II

SCENE 1

LIGHTS UP ON THE BEDROOM.

THE POET IS SITTING IN THE BED, HIS OWN, WATCHING A DRAMA ON TV. A REMOTE IS IN HIS HAND, A BOOK IN THE OTHER.

M1 TV   …I don't care.

M2 TV   We all have our roles to play, George. Just because you've stepped down doesn't mean the game doesn't go on. You know that. Someone has to keep the wolf from the gates.

M1 TV   I'd say it does.

M2 TV   Don't be a foo….

HE IDLY CHANGES CHANNELS, FLICKING FORWARD TO A NEWS PROGRAM. IT SUCCEEDS IN GAINING HIS ATTENTION.

NEWS TV   …where reports of continued unrest have been coming in. The earthquake, measuring 7.8 on the Richter scale, has been seen by some as the final nail in the coffin for the Korinov government. Government aid workers have continued to lobby for support but…

THERE'S A RING ON THE DOORBELL. HE SILENCES THE TV AND CHECKS HIS WATCH. THE DOORBELL RINGS AGAIN, INSISTENTLY.

HE RISES AND GOES TO THE DOOR, UNCON-
CERNED ABOUT HIS STATE OF DRESS.

ENTER SARAH, BREEZING PAST HIM INTO THE
ROOM.

SARAH   Did you see it?

POET   I'm watching it now. I didn't
think you were getting in til tomorrow.

SARAH   I've been here for a few days.
He's flying out tomorrow.

POET   (PROCESSING) OK.

SARAH   You answer the door like that?

POET   I wasn't expecting anyone.

SARAH   (LOOKING AT THE MUTED
TV) The stupid… If they'd just let the international
agencies in…

POET   Apparently they're beginning
to open up.

SARAH   Not fast enough. No government agencies. Only charities. Who the hell do they
think funds the charities in the first place?

POET   Strangely, I thought I did. You
didn't tell me you were getting in earlier.

SARAH   (AS THOUGH SEEING HIM
FOR THE FIRST TIME) Hey. Yeah, I'm sorry. I… I
hate lying. You know that. I thought it would be better for you…

POET   Don't worry about it. Come
here.

SHE SMILES AND MOVES INTO HIM, KISSING HIM PASSIONATELY.

SARAH   You smell of hotel bedsheets.

POET   Would you like to?

SARAH   (LAUGHING) Get off! I haven't... I need a shower.

POET   (HEADING OFF STAGE) What do you think they'll do?

EXIT POET.

SARAH STANDS WATCHING THE TV. PRESENTLY WE HEAR THE SOUND OF A SHOWER RUNNING.

SARAH   Let their people die. 7.8 and they all live in concrete bunkers. The death toll... I read the book.

ENTER POET.

POET   What was that?

SARAH   I read the book.

POET   Come in the shower with me.

SARAH   Did you hear what I said?

POET   I heard. Come in the shower with me.

SARAH   Don't you want to know if I liked it?

POET   Are you saying you didn't?

SARAH   A little obvious, don't you think?

POET   The themes?

SARAH   (SERIOUS) The   inscription.
It's…

POET   I thought you'd like it.

SARAH   I… I do, but… He's not stupid.

POET   He's never going to read it.

SARAH   And the people I work with?
The people you work with? They're not stupid e i -
ther. We've been out together. I've been your other
at award ceremonies. People…

POET   I don't care. I'm sorry. Yes.
You're right. People aren't stupid. Let them make of
it what they will. But please, don't ask me to care.

SARAH   You can be so naïve, sometimes.

POET   I wrote worlds for you and the
only thing you have to say about it is the inscription?

SARAH   You wouldn't understand.

POET   Maybe I understand too well.

SARAH   Silly bear. (PAUSE) I'm going.

POET   (CONFUSED) I just ran   the
shower…

SARAH   (POINTING TO THE TV) No,
there. I'm going there. We just got clearance.

POET   We.

SARAH   It's part of the mission. They're
giving clearance to the religious organizations
and…

POET   When.

SARAH   Tomorrow. We fly to Turkey
and then…

POET   This is what you came here for,
is it? To tell me?

SARAH   I wanted to see you.

POET   To tell me you were going there?
Great!

SARAH   Don't be so melodramatic!

POET   What if there's another earthquake? That's not out of the realm of possibility! And
the government? What if there's a coup?

SARAH   We're linked to the UN…

POET   What if they decide you're better to them as a western hostage? It's not like it's the
first time they've tried that trick.

SARAH   It's where the people are!

POET   It's too dangerous! He must be
out of his mind!

SARAH   They need help!

POET   Let him go! Let him preach hell-
fire and damnation to a people who just saw it
with their very eyes. Like that's going to go down
well.

SARAH   That's not what…

POET   Stay here. With me. Let him go.
You've done enough. Haven't you done enough?
I don't think I can stand another Zambia. Another

Zambia.

SARAH   It won't be like that.

POET   How in the name of hell would you know? Seriously. You can't promise me that! You can't! This… This is one of the most closed countries in the world, for god's sake. They don't have dissidents, they have martyrs.

SARAH   That has nothing to do…

POET   I can't. Seriously. I… I didn't know. In Zambia. No one told me! Do you understand that? No one told me. It was… I was at a party, for god's sake. I was at a party and this woman… This stupid woman started telling it like it was an anecdote. Weeks, weeks later. I had to sit there. I had to sit and listen as this stupid woman... Do you know what that did to me? Do you know? I couldn't reach…

SARAH   Hush.

POET   I can't go through that again. I…

SARAH   Hush now.

POET   I nearly jumped on a plane. Then and there. It was all I could…

SARAH   I have to go. Don't you see that? You think it would be any different for him…

POET   I don't care…

SARAH   But I do. I… I love you. And the book…

THE POET GETS UP AND STARTS TO MOVE UP-

STAGE, TOWARDS THE OUBLIETTE.

POET   Stay.

SARAH   You help the people in front of
you.

POET   I'm in front of you.

SARAH   It's not the same thing. You
don't need my help.

HE MOVES INTO THE OUBLIETTE. HEADING TO
HIS USUAL SPOT.

POET   I do. Really. I need it. I need
you.

SARAH   You can't have me.

POET   Why? Why is that? Why can't I
have you?

SARAH   Because I'm dead, silly.

END OF SCENE 1.

SCENE 2

LIGHTS DOWN ON THE BEDROOM. LIGHTS UP
ON THE OUBLIETTE.

THE POET IS WAKING, RECOVERING FROM
HIS DREAM. A FEW FEET AWAY THE JAILOR IS
STUDYING HIM CAREFULLY.

THE MISSIONARY IS ABSENT.

JAILOR   Good. You're awake.

POET   (LOOKING AROUND) Where is he?

JAILOR   I thought perhaps we would chat a little. In private.

POET   Where have you taken him?

JAILOR   He is quite safe. I have been asking around about you. You understand? It is not often a man buys himself into a jail cell. Out, yes. But not in.

POET   I have one more day.

JAILOR   He is a friend of yours? (SILENCE) No, I didn't think so. You do not act like a friend. My, how is it, my protégé, is that the right word?

POET   It'll do.

JAILOR   My protégé. He thinks he has treasure hidden. He thinks you buy your way in here to ask him about this treasure. He is young. He watches too many movies. (THE POET IS SILENT) I have been asking around about you. At the border, yes? They tell me you crossed without passport three weeks ago. They tell me you came illegally. Is this true?

POET   Does it matter?

JAILOR   To me? No. You want to crawl yourself into this hell hole, then fine. You have money, you can have service! This is the way of the world. Yes? You come to us and you say, let me in to see prisoner. Half now, half later. That is fine. This is the way. But I am thinking. I am thinking. How do we know you have more money. You come across border. This is great risk. You cannot bribe border guards. Ours, yes. Easy. But the other side? And yet, no passport when they search you. I think you do not want to be known.

TOO LATE THE POET NOTICES THAT HIS BAG HAS BEEN MOVED. THE JAILOR HAS BEEN THROUGH IT.

JAILOR(cont)   So, question I ask myself. How you know he is here. Answer is money. Of course. But you know where! You know who to ask. This is exceptional. You are not soldier, you are not spy!

POET   Is that right?

JAILOR   No. You are not spy. No craft. No... You come here. Loud. Money everywhere. This is good. This is the right way, but you do not hide it. Or cannot. No, no spy. That is not important. Besides, we have him three months. You know? There is no secret in him.

POET   And yet you continue to torture him.

JAILOR   Which you mind? Yes?

POET   If he knows nothing...

JAILOR   You have money. You are smart. But you are risk. Great risk. Coming in here. This is special prison. Geneva Convention? This does not fly. Outside world knows they create problems, I think. Perhaps for me?

POET   The outside world doesn't care

about anything you do. No oil!

JAILOR   Indeed. No oil! Still risk. Maybe when you leave I take money and kill you? I don't. But is risk nonetheless. Yes?

POET   Spit it out.

JAILOR   Boy, he watches TV. Me, I read. I read you. Long time ago. I almost forget. I lived in New York. Cab driver. You believe that? Five years! Long time ago. New life.   My daughter there. But I miss the old country. You understand that? No. I don't think you do. You have no country, do you? No country, no money, treasure. No secrets. So I think to myself, what is there? No money, no country, no secrets. Someone? Yes? Someone. (HE PULLS A BOOK FROM THE POET'S BAG) Her, someone? (SILENCE) You are romantic. You are hero. You love someone very much, I think. Not family. Not like this man. Not religion. I thought religion, but no. Not religion. Not god religion anyway. Woman. Woman, yes? His woman?

POET   What did you think of the meter? I was never happy with the meter?

JAILOR   You know nothing of what happens here. You know nothing of what happens to this man. You worship, yes, but not god. Woman! What kind of fool is that?

POET   The kind that doesn't torture other people.

JAILOR   That right? You think so? What you think? You don't torture this man? Loving his woman? You know nothing of what happens here.

Nothing!

POET   Enlighten me.

JAILOR   What means this, please? En…

POET   Tell me.

JAILOR   You maybe write poem about me, yes?

POET   If you like.

JAILOR   If you like. I had woman. Wife. Daughter. I was government, you believe this? Long time ago. Then came the war. You know this? The war? I was government so they take my wife. My son. My daughter, she is at school, safe, but they take my wife. Kill her, yes? Easy. This is war, killing is easy. They take my son. Don't kill him. Take him. What are they thinking? What? Maybe they think war will go bad for them and better to, ah, blackmail, this is right? Blackmail?

POET   I'm sorry to hear that.

JAILOR   But, they win war. Ha! I am exile. I run. Like rabbit. Like father. I run. New York. New life. But my son. My son, he is here. Somewhere, I think. I think. He is maybe alive. He is not, but I think it. So I return. It is five years, yes? Government changed, once, twice, three… Bad place. We are… Too much history. Too many memories. Sides. My grandfather town attack your grandfather town. Let's war! I search for him. I find records. This, we are good at! Records! I think you find that, yes? A remainder of communism. He is alive for two years. Two years. What they do with him in this time? I don't know. He is six. Why keep him alive? Then he is dead. Bullet. Gone. And I am here. This is our story. This is our history. You understand?

POET   I understand.

JAILOR   No. I think you don't. To you we are… amoral. That is your word. (HE TAPS THE BOOK) Here. Amoral! No Genève code. No goodness. We are backward country the world tries to forget!

POET   This man. The man you are imprisoning. The man you torture. He cared. When the earthquake…

JAILOR   Ah, the earthquake! Yes. Drama! To you, this is drama. This is shame. Poor people. Now they must open their borders! Now they must welcome the world. Forty years until communism. Did you come then? For that earthquake? Did you come for the camps? For our fathers? Tell me, what can you do more about? God's hand on earth or man's hand on our necks? I do not judge you. I live in America too. (PAUSE) You go now.

POET   I'm not ready.

JAILOR   If he does not tell you where she is now, he is not likely to.

POET   I have one more day!

JAILOR   (PREPARING TO LEAVE) Suit yourself (HE RAPS ON THE DOOR) Find her soon, is my advice. Today we try new torture. I do not think he lives after that.

FOOTSTEPS ARE HEARD COMING TOWARDS

HIM.

POET   Why? Why? He knows nothing. Nothing you don't already?

THE JAILOR LOOKS AT HIM AS IF THE QUESTION IS STRANGE.

JAILOR   The boy must learn. (THEN AS IF TO CLARIFY) Protégé? The boy must learn!

THE DOOR OPENS AND THE PROTÉGÉ PUSHES THE MISSIONARY INTO THE CELL AHEAD OF HIM, HIS HANDS BOUND. HE FALLS HARD TO THE FLOOR.

JAILOR   Two hours. Two hours then we start. (BEAT) Before lunch.

THE PROTÉGÉ GIGGLES AND THE PAIR LEAVE THE ROOM.

THE MISSIONARY LETS OUT A HOWL OF DESPERATION.

POET   Stop! Sandy. Stop. Look at me. What the hell's…

MISSIONARY   Leave me alone.

POET   Stop it!

MISSIONARY   This…

POET   Sandy!

MISSIONARY   No! This is what they do to religion…

POET   Listen!

MISSIONARY   They bleed it! They burn it! Beat

it out of you!

POET   Sandy!

MISSIONARY   The great atheist! The humanitarian.

POET   What the hell are you talking
about?

MISSIONARY   Two hours…

POET   I… They're cleaning the cell.
That's all. Stop it. They're cleaning the cell! God, I
don't know, someone's coming I suppose. That's
why I can't stay here after tomorrow. There're important people coming. They're reviewing your case!

MISSIONARY   Get away from me!

POET   They're reviewing your case.
They were just telling me. I think they'll let you go.

PAUSE.

SILENCE.

POET(cont)   Sandy…

MISSIONARY   You're a good friend, Peter.
You're a good friend. You were a good friend to her.
I know that. Here. After Zambia. You were a good
friend.

POET   We… I never… We weren't trying to hurt you.

MISSIONARY   You're a good friend. A good
friend.

POET   I'm… She loved you. It's...

MISSIONARY   Yes.

POET   That was never in doubt.

MISSIONARY   No.

POET   I was...

MISSIONARY   You're a good friend.

POET   She was never going to leave you.

MISSIONARY   (SIGH) This is what they do to men of faith. This is what they do! We believe so they break us. They beat us. This is what they do. You're the humanist. How can you not believe in truth that has to be beaten out of you?

SILENCE.

POET   I suppose... What made you decide? You know, to believe? What made you... I mean...

MISSIONARY   My Damascus moment?

POET   Yes.

MISSIONARY   I was... I was young. Youth. You believe anything when you're young. You believe people in power, your teachers, your betters... You think they must be better than you. Smarter. You believe anything when you're young. Is that hope, do you think? That what youth is? Hope. (BEAT) I was baptised at fifteen. I went to seminary... Now, when I think about what I believe, why I believe... Faith is the belief in something other than yourself. Something you can't truly know. Something... bigger. I suppose it could be anything. We all believe,

Peter. I just happen to believe in God. (BEAT) These things… I don't think I could live in a world without God. I don't think I could stand it. (PAUSE) You?

DURING THE MONOLOGUE THE POET MOVES DOWN INTO THE LOWER PART OF THE STAGE – THE BEDROOM – IN CLEAR VIEW OF THE AUDIENCE.

THE SOUNDS OF BOMBING ARE HEARD.

LIGHT DOWN ON THE OUBLIETTE. LIGHTS UP ON THE BEDROOM.

END OF SCENE 2.

SCENE 3

THE POET PACES THE ROOM, PAUSING TO LISTEN TO THE SOUND OF BOMBING FROM AFAR, WORRIED IT'S DRAWING CLOSER.

HE CHECKS HIS WATCH SEVERAL TIMES IN CONCERN.

THERE'S A KNOCK AT THE DOOR AND HE HURRIES TO OPEN IT.

FLYING INTO HIS ARMS, SARAH BURSTS THROUGH THE DOOR. THE COUPLE KISS WORRIEDLY AND PASSIONATELY AS THEY TALK, OVERLAPPING.

SARAH   What are you doing here?

POET   I thought you weren't coming.

SARAH   It's not safe.

POET   I've come to get you out.

SARAH   (EASING) What?

POET   Out. I've come to get you out. (THE COUPLE DISENGAGE) It's too dangerous here. They're taking the capital. If they take the airport we might never get out. I've got some friends with the American Embassy...

SARAH   I thought they'd all pulled out already?

POET   Non-essentials. These are... We'd be flying out with the army, basically. But it's still under diplomatic....

SARAH   I can't just go.

POET   Of course you can. You can.

SARAH   Sandy...

POET   He'll be fine. Honestly. The missions are going to pull everyone out.

SARAH   He's not in the city.

POET   (FRUSTRATED)   He's...   I can't... Sandy's a big boy, Sarah...

SARAH   Why did you come?

POET   It's not safe, Sarah.

SARAH   I wish you hadn't come. Here of all places. I thought this time...

POET   Do you have things? Things

you want to collect?

SARAH   No.

POET   Nothing?

SARAH   Nothing. I'm too tired, Peter. I'm too tired … I'll go with you. If you still want me…

POET   They want us to stay here. In the hotel. They've got people here. So we just stay put and they'll come and get us.

SARAH   We should never have come here. It's not… They're evil. I really think that. They're evil.

POET   You're shattered.

SARAH   How long can you live with injustice before you become unjust, do you think? We did good. At first. There's… There's a lot of poverty here, Peter. People have nothing. Nothing! We've failed them. Miserably. Politically, morally, we've failed them. Twenty years. That's how long they had democracy here. Free trade. (SHE LAUGHS) Twenty years and they're rejecting us completely. It's so stupid.

POET   We've got a little time.

A BOMB EXPLODES, MUCH CLOSER NOW. THERE'RE FOOTSTEPS IN THE HALL, PEOPLE SHOUTING, RUNNING. THE PAIR LISTEN.

SARAH   In Africa…

POET   Don't worry about it.

SARAH   When I was… When they attacked us. You could understand it, you know? This was… This was how it was, with people. This was… They made their living like this. Road blocks. This little hundred metres of road. This is how they made their money. We just didn't have any.

POET   Don't think about it.

SARAH   It was my idea, you know, to go round. It was my idea.

POET   Hush.

SARAH   We had money. I don't know why I said that. We had money. But it was donation money, you know. For the school.

POET   It's over now.

SARAH   So I said, sure, drive round. I… I thought I was being so clever. We'd saved… Then… I didn't even hear it. The blast. Just… Everything was red and the truck was being thrown. You know? Like a rag. Almost casually… He was… He annoyed me so much, you know that? Always chewing this to-bacco leaf. Over and over. It used to drive me crazy. And I killed him.

POET   They killed him. They did. They put the roadside bomb there. Not you. You didn't kill anyone.

SARAH   Poor Peter. You're so lost here, aren't you? Like a child really.

POET   It's you I'm worried about.

SARAH   Like a little boy. You shouldn't have to see this. Not you. I love you. You know that? I always have. Right from the very first moment. So… beautiful. Like you   didn't belong to the real world.

POET   I think they're getting closer.

SARAH   There's this boy. Kinhio. He's…
You should see this kid, Peter, he's… He reminds
me of you a lot. You know what I mean? He's with
Sandy.

POET   Then he'll be fine.

SARAH   You shouldn't have to see this.
You should stay like you are. You shouldn't exist.
Not here. Not here.

POET   Sarah, I need you to listen to
me now. Are you listening? We're getting out of
here, alright? Whatever's happened, we're getting
out of here. I promise. We're getting out of here. OK?

SARAH   Yes. Of course. Yes. You always
came for me. Didn't you? No matter where I was.

POET   You came for me too.

SARAH   Really?

POET   In the ways that count. Yes. You
did.

SARAH   Good. (BEAT) Good.

POET   Is there… I hesitate to ask this…
is there any way to get word, to Sandy?

SARAH   He's out of the capital. The
boy… I'm not even sure where. He was trying to
get… We've got this boy, at the office, and the pen-
icillin here is just, well… Out of date is the word, I
suppose. There's this man he knows, in Kurvet. He's
a trader, black market, and he thinks he can get some

for us, but I have no idea where he's meeting him.

POET   There's no one with a contact number?

SARAH   Poor Peter. No. There's no contact number. It's… He's been gone five days already but getting back into the city… You know how this thing started? The   real thing, I mean, not the thing on the news. There was a car accident. Simple as that. A car accident. Minister of something or other but it was a hit and run and the government thought it was the militants, so they start cracking down and the next thing… This. Stupid, isn't it? I get hit by a roadside bomb and it's just another day at the office. A minister crosses the road without looking both ways and we're smack bang in the middle of a war.

A MOBILE PHONE STARTS TO RING FROM SOMEWHERE ON THE BED. THEY BOTH JUMP AND THE POET STARTS TO RUMMAGE AROUND, LOOKING FOR IT.

POET   Shit. They gave me this phone… (FINDING IT, HE OPENS IT AND HITS A BUTTON) Hello? (PAUSE) Right. Yes. (HE LOOKS AT HIS WATCH) Now? OK.

HE HANGS UP.

POET(cont)   Do you have your passport? (SHE SHAKES HER HEAD) They want you to talk to you. In the lobby. It's just a formality. They need… It's just a formality. They know who you are but they need to meet you.

SARAH   Now?

POET   They're waiting. Come on.

SARAH   No. No. Peter. You stay. They…
They'll want to ask me about Sandy. Personal things,
you understand? It's better that you stay. You'll only
start acting like a jealous lover and we don't have the
time. You stay. I'm sure it's nothing. I'll be a couple
of minutes. Are you packed?

POET   I didn't bring anything.

SARAH   I'll only be a couple of minutes.
OK?

POET   OK.

SHE KISSES HIM.

SARAH   OK. It's for the best.

POET   Call the room if there's any
problem.

SARAH   I love you. You know that?

POET   I love you too. Call me if you
need anything.

SHE TURNS FOR THE EXIT AND HE TURNS TO
THE WINDOW, FOCUSING ON THE STREET
OUTSIDE. SHE WATCHES HIM FOR THE LAST
TIME, AND THEN EXITS.

WE HEAR THE SOUND OF THE ELEVATOR AND
FOOTSTEPS HEADING TOWARDS THE DOOR.

THE POET STANDS THERE FOR A MINUTE, DIS-
TRACTED, THINKING. THEN HIS THOUGHTS
TURN BACK TO HER AND HE REALIZES SHE'S
JUST SAID GOODBYE FOR THE LAST TIME.

POET(cont)   Sarah!

LIGHTS DOWN ON THE BEDROOM. LIGHTS UP ON THE OUBLIETTE.

THE POET – OSTENSIBLY HURRYING AFTER HER – RETURNS UPSTAGE TO THE OUBLIETTE.

END OF SCENE 3.

SCENE 4

THE DOOR OPENS TO THE OUBLIETTE AS THE POET REACHES THE STAGE.

THE JAILOR ENTERS, CHECKING ON THE TWO MEN BEFORE USHERING IN THE PROTÉGÉ, WHO PUSHES AN ELECTRIC CHAIR THROUGH THE OPEN DOORWAY.

THE MISSIONARY REMAINS CALM AND MO-TIONLESS IN HIS CORNER, QUIETLY DEFIANT, BUT THE POET STEPS FORWARD QUICKLY, OPENING HIS MOUTH TO SPEAK, THE ANGER RISING IN HIM.

CALMLY BUT FIRMLY THE JAILOR HITS THE POET IN THE FACE. BLOOD EXPLODES FROM HIS MOUTH AND THE POET FALLS TO THE FLOOR, SHOCKED AS MUCH AS PAINED BY THE SUDDEN VIOLENCE.

THE PROTÉGÉ, GIGGLING, MOVES THE CHAIR

TO THE FRONT OF THE OUBLIETTE, NO MORE THAN A FOOT FROM THE EDGE.

THE POET ATTEMPTS TO RISE AND THE JAILOR PUTS HIM DOWN AGAIN WITH SEVERAL SWIFT BLOWS, THE SUDDEN AND BRUTAL VIOLENCE NEVER REFLECTING ON THE MAN'S CALM FACE.

ASSURED THAT THE POET WILL NOT TRY TO RISE AGAIN, THE MAN TURNS HIS ATTENTION TO THE MISSIONARY.

THE PROTÉGÉ GRABS THE MISSIONARY WHO STRUGGLES AGAINST HIM, DRAGGING HIM TO THE CHAIR, THE WEAKENED MAN EASILY OVERPOWERED BY THE STRONGER PROTÉGÉ.

THE POET STIRS AND THE JAILOR ADDRESSES HIM WHILST SECURING THE MISSIONARY TO THE CHAIR.

JAILOR   I warned you to leave. I did tell you. Yes? I read your book. Not all. But, yes, I did not like it. All this love, all this energy. Over what? A woman? How is that love? Eh? How is that right? I thought to myself, what if we all acted like this, yes? What if we were all this selfish, this… stupid. Where would we be? You love a woman. So what? Everyone loves a woman. You think this gives you rights in this world? You think this makes you honourable? But you have money, so do you help with it? Do you do good? You waste it. Waste it! On this woman. You waste words on a woman. Words, I can understand! Words cost air, but life? Money? No, this is not to be wasted.

POET   (WEAKLY) Leave him alone!

JAILOR   And then I thought. You were like the fat cats. The fat cats before the revolution! You wasted things. You wasted air and life and money on, what? Cars, gold, women? Stupid. This here. This chair is great American invention. Like you. Idea is simple.

HE NODS TO THE PROTÉGÉ WHO MAKES A CONNECTION AT THE BACK OF THE CHAIR, ELECTROCUTING THE MISSIONARY, PROPELLING HIS BODY RIGIDLY OUT OF THE CHAIR, HELD IN PLACE ONLY BY THE BRACES AT HIS WRISTS AND ANKLES.

POET   No!

THE CURRENT ONLY LASTS A COUPLE OF SECONDS BUT THE EFFECTS ARE DEVASTATING TO EVERYONE IN THE ROOM.

THE JAILOR CUTS THE POWER OFF AND THE MISSIONARY FALLS BACK INTO THE SEAT, BREATHING HEAVILY.

HE HAS NOT SCREAMED.

THE POET, STILL ON HIS HANDS AND KNEES, HAS TURNED HIS FACE AWAY.

THE PROTÉGÉ LOOKS UNCOMFORTABLE AT WHAT HE HAS DONE.

THE JAILOR REACHES OVER AND GRABS THE POET'S HAIR, FORCING HIM TO LOOK.

JAILOR   We must love one another and die. Is that it? Look. Look! This is what your love has done to the man. Look!

HE NODS AND THE PROTÉGÉ HITS THE CON-
NECTION AGAIN, SENDING THE MISSION-
ARY INTO ANOTHER SPASM.

THE POET TRIES TO REACH OUT AND IS HIT BY
THE JAILOR.

THIS TIME THE TROUBLED PROTÉGÉ RELENTS
ON HIS OWN AND THE MISSIONARY FALLS
BACK INTO THE CHAIR CLOSE TO PASSING
OUT, AND VOMITS UNCONTROLLABLY.

THE JAILOR TURNS ON THE PROTÉGÉ.

JAILOR (cont)   (CALMLY) Why did you stop?

PROTÉGÉ   Id ist… (SWITCHING TO ENG-
LISH TO COPY THE JAILOR) I didn't know how
long.

JAILOR   How long, I say. OK?

POET   Leave him alone.

JAILOR   Leave who? The boy? The boy
must be trained, yes? This is for the state, you under
stand? The state. We will have prisoners soon. Really prisoners. With information. You understand?
The boy must learn. This is not so powerful. You
understand? Like a light, yes? Nothing more. Look.
(HE SPEAKS TO THE MISSIONARY) Are you alright, Alessandro? Yes? See. He is alive. He is fine.
The boy must learn. Beatings are good. Beatings and
loneliness will break a man. It is not so complicated.
Hopelessness and pain. In that order. That is what
will break a man. But beatings. Beatings will leave a
man black, yes? Like this! Some this is fine. Others,
this will not do. Great American invention. Electrici-

ty.

MISSIONARY   (HORSELY) Titus.

THE JAILOR IS SHOCKED TO HEAR HIS NAME
AND HE LEANS FORWARD TO LISTEN, EMBAR-
RASSED THAT THE MAN KNOWS HIS NAME.

JAILOR   Yes?

MISSIONARY   I forgive you, Titus.

THE JAILOR IS ANGERED. EMOTION SHOWS IN
HIS FACE FOR THE FIRST TIME.

HE STANDS BACK, THINKING, THEN HEADS TO
THE POET.

JAILOR   And you. Do you, how did he
say, forgive me?

POET   (BITTERLY) No.

THIS CALMS THE JAILOR.

JAILOR   Good. Good. This is good. But,
the boy must learn. He is weak, aren't you boy?
Yes. Weak. He likes suffering, but not pain. He likes
hurting but not giving hurt. He is cruel. Cruel is not
good. You must not hate. Hate is emotion. You must
not hate. He is weak, yes? But we will teach him,
poet. Will we not? He needs a teacher. Poet. You will
teach.

POET   Go to hell.

IN ONE SWIFT MOVE THE JAILOR BRINGS
HIS BATON DOWN ON THE POET'S KNEE. HE
SCREAMS IN AGONY AND WRITHES IN PAIN.

JAILOR   You will teach him. One way or

the other. (HE MOTIONS TO THE PROTÉGÉ) Hold him.

THE PROTÉGÉ MOVES OVER AND GRIPS THE POET FROM BEHIND, PULLING HIM UP.

CALMLY AND WITHOUT MALICE THE JAILOR STRIKES HIM ACROSS THE FACE.

THE PROTÉGÉ PREVENTS HIM FROM FALLING AND THE JAILOR KNEELS IN FRONT OF HIM.

JAILOR   You are writer, yes? Poet?

HE NODS AT THE PROTÉGÉ AND HE HOLDS OUT THE POET'S LIMP HAND. THE POET, SEE-ING WHAT'S ABOUT TO HAPPEN STRUGGLES BUT IS HELD FIRM.

THE JAILOR BREAKS HIS FINGER.

THE POET SCREAMS IN AGONY.

JAILOR   Do not pass out on me, Mister Famous Poet. I need you to be a teacher now. I need you to show the boy how is done, yes? I need you to teach him about pain. About always causing pain.

HE DRAGS THE POET OVER TO THE CONNEC-TION SWITCH AT THE BACK OF THE CHAIR, PLACING HIS FOOT PAINFULLY ON THE PO-ET'S HAND. THE POET WRITHES IN PAIN.

JAILOR   I need you to teach us. Teach us about causing pain, yes? Teach us!

POET   (WEAKLY) No.

THE JAILOR INCREASES THE PRESSURE ON THE HAND. THE POET SCREAMS.

JAILOR   It is not so hard. Yes? A simple switch.

HE INCREASES THE PRESSURE AGAIN.

JAILOR   Teach us.

POET   Please!

THE JAILOR TWISTS HIS FOOT AND WE HEAR THE BONES BREAK. THE POET SCREAMS.

JAILOR   No, no pleases! Teach us.

THE POET REACHES OVER AND FLICKS THE SWITCH, SENDING THE MISSIONARY INTO A SPASM.

HE DOES NOT STOP UNTIL THE JAILOR NODS.

JAILOR   (TO THE PROTÉGÉ) There. See! That was teaching. Good teaching! You see? How easy it is to cause pain.

HE RELEASES THE HAND FROM UNDER HIS FOOT AND KNEELS BEFORE THE BROKEN POET.

JAILOR   Now. Do it again.

THE POET OBEYS, SENDING THE MISSIONARY FAR OUT OF HIS SEAT, THE BONDS STRAINING AS HE WRITHES IN PAIN.

THEN, SUDDENLY, THEY BREAK AND THE MISSIONARY FALLS FORWARD, PROPELLED OFF THE EDGE OF THE CLIFF, FALLING TO THE BED BELOW AS THE LIGHTS FALL ON THE OUBLIETTE.

END OF SCENE 4.

SCENE 5

A SINGLE WEAK SPOT HOLDS THE MISSION-
ARY AS HE LIES INERT ON THE BED.

SARAH ENTERS, QUIETLY REMOVING HER
SHOES SO AS NOT TO WAKE HER SLEEPING
HUSBAND.

THE MISSIONARY TURNS IN THE BED, STILL
ONLY LIT WITH THE SOFT SPOT, AND REACHES
FOR A LIGHT SWITCH.

LIGHTS UP ON THE BEDROOM.

THE MISSIONARY IS CHANGED, HIS FACE UN-
MARKED, HIS DAMAGED EYE OPEN FOR THE
FIRST TIME.

SARAH   Hey, sorry. I didn't want to
wake you.

MISSIONARY   S'ok.

SARAH SITS ON THE SIDE OF THE BED, TOUCH-
ING HIM INTIMATELY.

HE SMILES UP AT HER.

MISSIONARY(cont) You just getting in?

SARAH   Go back to sleep.

MISSIONARY   What time is it?

SARAH   Four. Go back to sleep. I like
watching you sleep.

MISSIONARY   How was your trip?

SARAH   Good. I think. The funding is secure, that's the main thing. They can even build the storage container, I think. As long as it comes through.

MISSIONARY   I was writing a sermon. Must have fallen asleep.

SARAH   What's it about?

MISSIONARY   I wanted to do something on Ruth. The women here…

SARAH   Sandy…

MISSIONARY   You OK?

SARAH   Do you… I have something I need to tell you? I wasn't going to but…

MISSIONARY   What's this about?

SARAH   I'd… Do you remember Peter? Peter Armitage?

MISSIONARY   Is he a contributor?

SARAH   No. Well, yes. Sort of. I met him again. He's a poet. I think I've told you about him. We grew up together. Back home. His family had a summer house near my parents…

MISSIONARY   I think I remember.

SARAH   He was at the hotel.

MISSIONARY   On the island?

SARAH   Yes. He was giving a lecture. You know. One of those literary getaways. He's quite famous.

MISSIONARY   (CAREFULLY) It's nice to catch up with old friends.

SARAH   You know we used to be… Before we met… I didn't want you to find out. Accidentally. I didn't want you to…

MISSIONARY   (SUDDENLY ACTIVE) I was talking with Mark, about Zambia. The school. He thinks it's a good idea. Education-wise alone, he thinks it's a good idea. They're going to hold a board meeting and look at funds, but it's exactly the kind of the thing we set the mission up for in the first place so I don't see there being a problem. He's thinking April. At the latest, April. There's all the shots and… AIDS is a problem. Not with the shots, naturally. I mean with the education. What's the life expectancy! But he thinks the council will go for it and there's so much we can do. So much we can do, you know.

SARAH   It's not important.

MISSIONARY   (BEAT) It's the only thing that's important. Nothing else matters. Not you, not me. God provides for us so that we can… Nothing else matters.

SILENCE.

SARAH   I understand.

MISSIONARY   We have no right to happiness. No right to it. I mean… This is what you wanted. What you asked for? Zambia? The school?

SARAH   Very much so.

MISSIONARY   We have no right to happiness.

There is nothing in the Bible about being happy. Nothing at all. I remember thinking... How often have you said that? How often? The people we put in front of us.

SARAH   I'm your wife!

MISSIONARY   That's exactly what I mean.

SARAH   I missed you. I just... I wanted to let you know that.

MISSIONARY   (GOING TO HER) Come here.

SARAH GOES TO HIM.

THE PAIR KISS CALMLY, SADLY, AND INTIMATELY. THE KISSING ACCELERATES INTO A PASSIONATE EMBRACE AND THE PAIR FALL BACK ON THE BED.

A SOFT SPOT LIGHTS THE OUBLIETTE. THE CHAIR HAS GONE. THE POET SQUATS ON THE EDGE OF THE CLIFF, LOOKING DOWN ON THE LOVERS IN THE BED.

POET   I don't believe you.

MISSIONARY   I don't care.

POET   She loved me.

MISSIONARY   There are more important things than love.

POET   How did she die?

MISSIONARY   It was nothing... She walked in on a robbery. Of all the... There were looters. Lots of looters. When an army is invading a city there are always looters. She walked into the shop. The door was

open so she probably thought it was open for business. So many shops were closed at that time. With
the army coming. She probably looked at a hundred
shops before she found that one. She just walked in
and they shot her. Just like that. I was out of the city
at the time. They were evacuating the embassies and
I couldn't get back in time. So pointless. So…

POET   I'm sorry… For your loss. I'm
sorry for your loss.

THE TWO FALL BACK INTO THEIR LOVEMAK-
ING.

LIGHTS FALL ON THE BEDROOM.

THE POET REMAINS WHERE HE IS, LOOKING
OUT DOWN AT THE MEMORY OF THE MISSION-
ARY, OR PERHAPS HIS IMAGINATION.

EVENTUALLY HE STANDS AND WALKS BACK-
WARDS INTO THE DARKNESS.

THE SOFT SPOT FADES TO BLACK.

END OF SCENE 5.

SCENE 6

LIGHTS UP ON THE OUBLIETTE.

THE TWO MEN ARE SITTING IN THEIR REGU-
LAR SPOTS, THE MISSIONARY MORE SLUMPED
THAN USUAL.

THE POET IS TEARING A SHIRT FROM HIS BAG TO MAKE A BANDAGE FOR HIS HAND.

POET   She called me you know. After. When they'd closed the border.

THE MISSIONARY NODS.

POET   She told me she was sorry.

MISSIONARY   I wasn't there.

POET   She said. I think... She was careless. Concerned. About you. She wanted me to put pressure on... whoever... She said you were involved with the black market. She...

MISSIONARY   I know.

POET   I think it might be why they arrested you.

MISSIONARY   They played me the tape. In Kubari. Before. It doesn't matter.

POET   I suppose not.

MISSIONARY   How's your hand?

POET   Bad.

MISSIONARY   Welcome to the world.

SILENCE.

MISSIONARY(cont) You never read me any of your poetry.

POET   (SMILING WANLY) I didn't want to torture you.

THE MISSIONARY SMILES.

MISSIONARY   Sleep, I think.

THE POET LOOKS AT HIM AND NODS, NOTHING LEFT TO SAY. THE MISSIONARY FALLS ASLEEP. THE POET MOVES ACROSS AND COVERS HIM MORE ADEQUATELY WITH THE BLANKET.

THE PEEP-HOLE OPENS AND THE JAILOR LOOKS IN BEFORE ENTERING, THE POET'S BOOK IN HIS HAND.

ENTER JAILOR.

JAILOR   You will need this, I think. Per-haps at the border.

THE POET TAKES THE BOOK SILENTLY.

JAILOR(cont)   You fear me now. This is good. This is right. Yes?

POET   What happened to the boy?

JAILOR   Protégé? He is gone. Home. This is not his life. Perhaps you will feel good about this, yes? Time for you to go.

POET   Let him go.

JAILOR   That, I cannot do. Inspection comes. There must be body. There must be prisoner, yes? Otherwise I am not jailor, I think.

POET   You don't need him anymore.

JAILOR   That is not for me to decide. You wonder, perhaps, why him? Why I use him? Not others?

POET   The thought had crossed my mind.

JAILOR   Religion is bad. It makes people

strong. Strong enough to die. Not fear death. Harder to break. Harder to understand. You think this too, I think.

POET   That's no reason.

JAILOR   (SHRUGGING) Better one man than three. Other men die by now, I think. Give up. You go now. Yes? One in, one out. No more torture for him. This I swear.

POET   One in, one out.

PAUSE.

JAILOR   Ah, you poets. So romantic. You torture this man. You nearly kill him.

POET   Please.

THE JAILOR STUDIES HIM, THEN RAPS ON THE DOOR.

ENTER GUARD.

JAILOR   You are sure?

THE POET NODS. THE JAILOR MOTIONS TO THE GUARD AND HE LIFTS THE MISSIONARY TO HIS FEET, WAKING HIM ENOUGH TO WALK SLUGGISHLY BUT NOT ENOUGH TO RECOGNIZE WHAT'S GOING ON.

AS HE GOES TO EXIT THE POET STUFFS THE POEM HE WAS WORKING ON INTO THE DAZED MAN'S POCKET.

THE JAILOR MOTIONS AGAIN AND THE GUARD LEADS THE MISSIONARY OUT INTO THE CORRIDOR.

JAILOR(cont)   How is your hand?

POET   Broken.

JAILOR   I will get you something, yes? If you are to stay here. Perhaps you will write?

HE STEPS OUT OF THE DOOR, CLOSING IT BE-HIND HIM.

THE POET ALONE IN THE CELL LISTENS TO THE FOOTSTEPS, THEN THE ELEVATOR.

HE PICKS UP THE BOOK WITH HIS GOOD HAND AND MAKES HIS WAY TO THE EDGE OF THE CLIFF, LOOKING DOWN AT THE DROP BELOW, TRYING TO SEE THE MISSIONARY LEAVING.

PAINFULLY BUT DELIBERATELY HE BEGINS TO TEAR PAGES FROM THE BOOK, THROWING THEM OUT ON THE WIND WHERE THEY DRIFT INTO THE DISTANCE.

POET   (SOTTO) Sarah.

HE TURNS, TAKING STEPS BACK INTO THE CELL, THEN TURNS AGAIN AND, RUNNING, FLINGS HIMSELF OFF THE EDGE OF THE CLIFF AS THE LIGHTS COME DOWN.

BLACKOUT.

SCENE 7

LIGHTS UP ON THE BEDROOM.

IT IS WEEKS LATER. WE HEAR THE NOISE OF A
PLANE DEPARTING NOISILY FROM NEARBY.

PAUL, AN ENVOY OF THE AMERICAN EMBAS-
SY, LEADS THE MISSIONARY INTO THE HOTEL
ROOM. THE MISSIONARY, STILL PALE AND
BRUISED, IS ON THE MEND, HIS EYE LARGELY
HEALED.

PAUL   Here you go.

MISSIONARY   Thank you.

PAUL   Not at all.

MISSIONARY   I'm sorry. I... Your name. I've
forgotten...

PAUL   Paul.

MISSIONARY   Thank you, Paul. And please
thank your embassy for me. Everyone has been...

PAUL   Not at all, sir. We're more than
glad to help one of our friends. The flight doesn't
leave for a few hours, sir. We're sorry about that.
Flights here aren't exactly an exact science, if you
know what I mean? There's a shower here if you
want one, though I wouldn't bet too highly on hot
water. Room service is passable though, sir. I'd stay
away from anything uncooked, but the burgers are
pretty good. Would you like me to order something
for you before...

MISSIONARY   No. No. Thank you. Thank you.

PAUL   No problem. Well, I guess I'll
leave you alone. The, um, the mission has insisted
on picking up the tab for this, sir, so there's no problem checking out. A car will take you directly to the

plane, they'll give you a call here, and you just meet them in the lobby, alright?

MISSIONARY   Thank you, Paul. You've been very kind. Very kind.

PAUL   Not at all, sir. After what you've been through… Well, I'll leave you alone.

PAUL HEADS TO THE DOOR AND STOPS.

PAUL(cont)   If I can just say, sir? We're all going to miss her, sir. Mrs. Menine. These months she's been with us. Well, she's been great. I just wanted to say that. The perfect guest. She… They wanted to send her home, sir. When we lost word of you. She wouldn't go, sir. Said she'd take American citizenship before leaving the embassy. I just wanted to say that, you know. She's been… Well, she's an inspiration to us all, sir.

ENTER SARAH.

MISSIONARY   Thank you, Paul.

PAUL (TURNING TO GO) Ma'am.

SARAH   Paul.

EXIT PAUL.

SARAH   (TO MISSIONARY) Where do you think you're going?

MISSIONARY   I thought it was…

SARAH   Sit! You know what the doctor told you. Let me look at you. See. You're healing already. You are healing, right?

MISSIONARY   Of course.

SARAH   We've got a couple of minutes. Kinhio says he'll meet us at the airport. If you
hadn't… It's a miracle really, all of it…

MISSIONARY   Sarah…

SARAH   And when we get to London…

MISSIONARY   Sarah. Stop.

SARAH   Are you alright?

MISSIONARY   I'm… Yes, I'm fine. I've… I've
decided to leave the mission.

SARAH   Well, London…

MISSIONARY   The Mission, the church, all of
it. Everything. I'm… I don't think I believe in it anymore.

SARAH   It's   only   natural,   after
everything…

MISSIONARY   I don't mean that. I mean it. All
of it. This isn't what I believe in anymore. All this.

SARAH   What then?

MISSIONARY   You. I believe in you. In us. I
want… I want to be selfish. I want to believe in you!

ENTER PAUL, KNOCKING BEFORE ENTERING.

PAUL   Hi. Sorry. They're ready for
you, sir.

THE PAIR RISE AND START TO COLLECT THEIR
THINGS. SARAH MOVES AHEAD OF THE MIS-
SIONARY AS THEY HEAD OUT OF THE ROOM.

PAUL(cont)   We've spoken with the press as

well as we can manage it. I think they're going to leave you alone, but you should be prepared for a few flash bulbs upon landing…

EXIT SARAH AND PAUL.

THE MISSIONARY DIGS OUT THE PIECE OF PA-PER THE POET GAVE HIM BEFORE HE LEFT. HE LOOKS AT IT AND THEN TOSSES IT ON THE BED.

LIGHTS DOWN ON THE ROOM.

LIGHTS UP ON THE OUBLIETTE.

WE HEAR THE POET READING ALOUD IN THE EMPTY CELL.

POET (OFF)

The Lords of Shouting and I rise early these days.

Ten million and one eyes looking eastward in expec-tation

Of the sun. Voices, voicing volumes, chasing

The sun skyward in the futile fulfilment of another dawn.

And I, waiting for a different call, the telephone still

On the bedside table, the letter undelivered, a pen

With the ink still in.

Satisfied, the Lords of Shouting retire into another

Morn, and I, to bed, belittled by another night

Where the sun never rises, the phone never rings

And my mind finds feelings in the most

Meaningful of myths.

LIGHTS DOWN.
CURTAIN.
THE END.

Also by

THOMAS ALEXANDER

THOMAS ALEXANDER

cover design by Snipfrog

THE VISITOR

THE VISITOR

BY

THOMAS ALEXANDER

WHEN THE LOVER OF A FAMOUS WRITER GOES MISSING IN A WAR RAVAGED COUNTRY, HE BRIBES HIS WAY INTO A JAIL TO QUESTION HER HUSBAND, A MISSIONARY, WHO IS BEING TORTURED AS A TRAINING EXERCISE BY HIS CAPTORS.

ALONE IN THE CELL, THE TWO START A DIALOGUE ABOUT THE NATURE OF BELIEF.

BELIEF IN GOD, LOVE AND POLITICS.

MURDER ME GENTLY

By

THOMAS ALEXANDER

cover design by SimplA Photography by Chris Boland

"ONE MAN... ONE WOMAN... AND THE QUEST FOR JUSTICE IN AN UNJUST WORLD"

MODERN DAY RUSSIA THROUGH THE MEDIUM OF FILM NOIR

BLENDING REAL LIFE EVENTS WITH COMEDY AND INTRIGUE, *MURDER ME GENTLY*'S UNIQUE PERSPECTIVE ON THE WORLD OF RUSSIAN POLITICS AS SEEN THROUGH THE LENS OF FILM NOIR, SPANS THE ASSASSINATION OF INTERNATIONALLY RENOWNED JOURNALISTS, PUTIN'S REACH FOR THE RETURN OF SOVIET SATELLITE STATES, AND THE INFILTRATION OF GOVERNMENT BY OLIGARCHS AND CRIMINALS.

PROVIDING A DAMMING INDICTMENT OF THE WEST'S INABILITY TO HALT MOSCOW'S POLICY OF EXPANSIONISM *MURDER ME GENTLY* LENDS A THEATRICAL EXPOSE TO THE VERY REAL WORLD OF CORRUPTION AND GREED IN INTERNATIONAL POLITICS TODAY.

A CONMAN, A DISGRACED INTERPOL AGENT, A MAFIA BOSS, A CIA SPOOK, AND THE SECRET TO THE FUTURE ALL UNITE IN AN UNLIKELY ALLIANCE IN A LOVE AFFAIR THAT WILL DEFINE THE FATE OF THE WORLD IN THOMAS ALEXANDER'S

... MURDER ME ... GENTLY!

cover design by SimplyA

GRE∆T

GREAT

BY

THOMAS ALEXANDER

A REMOTE ROOM IN THE THROWS OF WINTER.

THE ONCE GREAT MAN LIVES ALONE NOW WITH HIS SON,

AN OLD FRIEND HAS COME TO VISIT. HE HAS CLIMBED UP FROM THE VILLAGE IN ORDER TO OFFER THE OLD MAN ONE LAST CHANCE TO ESCAPE THE ENCROACHING WINTER THAT IS ABOUT TO TAKE HIM, STIRRING UP MEMORIES OF BETTER TIMES AND THE WARMTH OF SUMMER.

BEGAT

By

THOMAS ALEXANDER

cover design by SimplyA

By Thomas Alexander

IN A COUNTRY, AFTER THE WAR, A JUDGE THROWS A DINNER PARTY, SEEKING SUPPORT AGAINST A POWERFUL MINISTER WHO HAS RAPED AND KILLED A SERVANT GIRL.

BUT THE JUDGE HIMSELF IS THE TARGET TONIGHT, AND THE SHADOW OF THE WAR HE SO DESPERATELY WANTS TO LEAVE BEHIND THREATENS TO ENGULF HIS FAMILY AS A YOUNG WOMAN SEEKS REVENGE FOR THE SINS OF HIS PAST.

cover design by SimplyA

A BR...

Happiness

NOT EVERY DOOR SHOULD BE OPENED.

HAPPINESS

BY

THOMAS ALEXANDER

ON A REMOTE HEADLAND IN NORTH WALES A MAN AND HIS PARAPLEGIC SON DREAM OF LIFE BEYOND THE CONFINES OF THEIR FOUR WALLS.

BUT WHEN A WOMAN OFFERS THEM THE ESCAPE THEY SO CRAVE THEY FIND THEY ARE BOUND BY MORE THEN THEIR DREAMS.

THE JEALOUSY OF A BORED POLICE-MAN AND THE KINDNESS OF A MAIL ORDER BRIDE SET THEM ON A PATH OF HOPE AND DESTRUCTION.

THE LAST CHRISTMAS

THE LAST
CHRISTMAS

BY

THOMAS ALEXANDER

IT'S NEWS!

cover design by SimplyA

WHEN AN EMBATTLED NEWSROOM RECEIVES A POTENTIALLY EARTH SHATTERING STORY MINUTES BEFORE AIR ON CHRISTMAS DAY THE CAREFUL EQUILIBRIUM OF THE TEAM IS SHATTERED AND OLD DIVIDING LINES COME TO THE FORE, TURNING CO-WORKER AGAINST CO-WORKER.

SET IN REAL TIME AND INCORPORATING ACTUAL AND INTERCHANGEABLE NEWS EVENTS THE LAST CHRISTMAS PITS SOCIAL POLITICS AGAINST JOURNALISTIC INTEGRITY IN A BATTLE OF THE ETHICS.

GOD

BY

THOMAS ALEXANDER

WHEN THE NAMED PARTNER OF A SMALL LAW FIRM DIES, LEAVING LARGE DEBT, THE REMAINING MISFITS OF THE FIRM ARE FORCED TO TAKE ON JUST ABOUT ANY CLIENT AVAILABLE, INCLUDING A LITIGIOUS SOCCER-MUM WHO WOULD LIKE TO SUE GOD FOR THE DEATH OF HER HUSBAND – HIT BY A LIGHTNING BOLT ON THE 15TH HOLE OF A MUNICIPAL GOLF COURSE.

THE TRIAL BECOMES COMPLICATED HOWEVER, WHEN AN INDIGENT WITH NO BACKGROUND AND A CANNY KNACK OF KNOWING EVERYONE'S BACKGROUND ENTERS THE COURTROOM CLAIMING TO BE 'GOD'.

BATTING BACK AND FORE BETWEEN THE COURTROOM AND THE PERSONAL LIVES OF THE LAWYERS, 'GOD' IS A FAST PACED COURTROOM DRAMA/COMEDY THAT USES ORIGINAL STAGING AND NON-LINEAR STORYTELLING TO PROVIDE A LIGHT-HEARTED, BUT COMPLEX SOCIAL DRAMA.

THE FAMILY

BY

THOMAS ALEXANDER

TODAY, FOR THE FIRST TIME IN LONGER THAN ANYONE CAN REMEMBER, THE FAMILY ARE GATHERING. THEY ARE GATHERING TO CELEBRATE THE ENGAGEMENT OF THE MATRIARCHAL NIECE, THEY ARE GATHERING TO CELEBRATE THE LAST BIRTHDAY OF THE PATRIARCH, THEY ARE GATHERING TO WELCOME HOME THE PRODIGAL SON AND HIS BEAUTIFUL GIRLFRIEND AND THEY ARE GOING TO CELEBRATE ALL THIS WITH A SLIDESHOW.

CANDID PHOTOGRAPHS. PHOTOGRAPHS OF THINGS NO ONE THOUGHT ANYONE ELSE KNEW ABOUT. PHOTOGRAPH TAKEN WHEN NO ONE ELSE WAS THERE.

IT'S ALL COMING OUT TODAY. IN BLACK AND WHITE FOR EVERYONE TO SEE. THE REMNANTS OF CHILD ABUSE, INFIDELITY, LOSS, DESTRUCTION AND MISSED BIRTHDAY PARTIES. IT'S ALL COMING OUT. IT'S GOING TO BE A LONG NIGHT. POSSIBLY FOREVER.

THE RECRUITMENT OFFICER

BY

THOMAS ALEXANDER

TOM, A CHARMING YANKEE RECRUITER, COMES TO AN UNSPECIFIED ENGLISH TOWN AND FALLS IN LOVE WITH THE CONFERENCE CENTRE MANAGER, JULIA.

BUT WHAT EXACTLY IS HE RECRUITING FOR? WHY DOES EVERYONE WHO JOINS NEVER COME BACK AND WHAT IS ON THE OTHER SIDE OF THE DOOR

WHERE DO THE RECRUITS GO AFTER SIGNING UP?

AN EXISTENTIAL LOVE STORY THAT ASKS QUESTIONS OF WHO WE ARE, WHAT WE WANT FROM LIFE AND WHETHER WE'RE GETTING IT, THE RECRUITMENT OFFICER IS A REMODELLING OF THE 1706 PLAY BY GEORGE FARQUHAR. *THE RECRUITING OFFICER*

Writer's Block

By

Thomas Alexander

Paul Block was once a prolific writer. A recipient of both the Pen and Faulkner awards and the author of over ten different novels, he was once considered the UK's most up and coming writer until, at the age of forty, he suffered a nervous breakdown.

Ten years later the world has forgotten Paul Block. Holed up in his study he has been working on the same first page of his new novel for nearly five years, kept company by only his maid, a foul mouthed Irish hit-man, a veteran of the battle of Gettysburg and a nineteen forties femme fetal.

Today, all that's going to change. Paul has a busy day ahead of him. First he's going to kill a persistent and charmless young reporter who wants to do a piece on 'writer's block' and then he's going to have a rare visit from his son who's bringing him bad news and a new couch.

With a missing body and a son who hates him, Paul must finally rid himself of his protagonists if he's ever going to stay out of jail, and finish that first page.

WRITING WILLIAM
BY
THOMAS ALEXANDER

"We want to put our education to use and our education is, was, and god damned always will be William fucking Shakespeare! We want lines we don't understand. We want plot holes so big you can drive a truck through them! We want to make sense of it all! Or at least understand what we studied it for in the first place! You want to put on a play? We want Shakespeare!"

Released in commemoration of Shakespeare's 450th anniversary this special edition of Writing William contains the original playbill and deleted scenes along with a new forward by Thomas Alexander.

Writing William follows a young, aspiring, playwright who, in order to get his work on stage, forges a Shakespeare play.

Basing the play on the relationship between Henry II and Eleanor of Aquitaine during the murder of Thomas Becket, Will, starts to see it mirror his own failing marriage as he struggles to find approval from an unforgiving spouse.

Backed by a working class billionaire and supported by an array of aging actors, the lead of which is mute, Will finds cathartic release in the writing of the play and it's impending production, but he hasn't taken into account just how gullible the theatre going public truly are.

cover design by SimplyA:

COMMEMORATIVE 450TH BIRTHDAY EDITION

A PLAY ABOUT LOVE, THEATRE & PLAGIARISM

Writing William

By

Thomas William.
Shakespeare Alexander

INCLUDES FORWARD BY AUTHOR
DELETED SCENES & ORIGINAL PLAYBILL

A comedic farce, Writing William blends Shakespearian dialogue with modern humour and innovative staging to look at the relationship of the artist and his art, the burden of success upon a relationship, and the true cost of producing a play.

THOMAS

Japan, 1945 – A Family At War

When a wandering priest escaping a troubled past is taken in by a prominent family, a quiet city in northern Japan is forced to confront the dark shadows of war seeping into their lives in ways they could never have anticipated.

With its townsmen scattered throughout the farthest ends of a desperate empire in a final defence against the encroaching West, the idyllic northern city of Morioka, far removed from the harsh realities of the front, is largely left to itself.

THOMAS ALEXANDER

A Scattering of Orphans

But when a prominent doctor is conscripted and sent to Manila, his sister is left as head of the household and must deal with a young priest living at the bottom of their garden with a large collection of maps and strange knowledge of English.

As the cold hand of war approaches, each person must choose their own destiny and place in the new world.

THE OTHER SIDE

ALEXANDER

Commemorating the 70th Anniversary of the end of WW2! A trilogy spanning the length of the war from the viewpoint of an ordinary Japanese family.

Thomas Alexander

The Disingenuous Martyr

omas Alexander

Beyond The Noonday Sun

Offering a unique perspective through the eyes of a rural Japanese family into the impact of history's bloodiest war to date, *A Scattering of Orphans* is one family's attempt to make sense of a changing world amidst the desolation of war, both home and abroad.

OF THE SUN